MOSAIC ORPHEUS

TITLES IN THE SERIES

MOSAIC ORPHEUS

Peter Dale Scott

McGill-Queen's University Press
Montreal & Kingston | London | Ithaca

© McGill-Queen's University Press 2009
ISBN 978-0-7735-3506-0

Legal deposit first quarter 2009
Bibliothèque nationale du Québec

Printed in Canada on acid-free paper that is 100% ancient forest free
(100% post-consumer recycled), processed chlorine free

McGill-Queen's University Press acknowledges the support of the
Canada Council for the Arts for our publishing program. We also
acknowledge the financial support of the Government of Canada
through the Book Publishing Industry Development Program (BPIDP)
for our publishing activities.

LIBRARY AND ARCHIVES CANADA CATALOGUING
IN PUBLICATION

Scott, Peter Dale
Mosaic Orpheus / Peter Dale Scott.

(Hugh MacLennan poetry series ; 20)
Poems.

ISBN 978-0-7735-3506-0
I. Title.   II. Series.

PS8587.C637M68 2009   C811'.54   C2008-906115-2

Typeset by Garet Markvoort in 10.5/13.5 Minion and Meta+

In memoriam Judith Stronach

CONTENTS

Seven Canadian Poems

We can still hear that high and sometimes irritatingly nasal note of whiny self-righteousness today among Canadians who, accepting the undoubted superiority of American military power, feel that their distinctive contribution to the alliance can and should be a quality in which Americans are poor, while Canada is specially, even uniquely rich – morality.
– Walter Russell Mead, *God and Gold*, 47

I'm a Canadian – that's good enough for me.
– Canon Frederick George Scott

THE POWER OF PRAYER

Hath not God made foolish the wisdom of this world?
– I Cor 1:20

People said my Uncle Arthur was a saint
he was very gentle
he absolutely never raised his voice

Such an odd contrast
to my grandfather the outgoing
Beloved Padre, who had inspired

thousands in the trenches of France
and whose church of St. Matthew's
on the ramparts of Upper Town

overlooked the vulgate people
with no reason to share
his faith in the British Empire

who had rioted against conscription
until sixty of them were shot
My grandfather willed that Arthur his young curate

should be married to his daughter my Aunt Mary
who to Arthur's confusion when they met
was disguised in men's clothes and smoking a pipe

There was trouble with the bishop of Quebec
something to do with High Church
candlesticks and incense

versus the *muscular Christianity*
that means business
And when my grandfather retired

they sent Uncle Arthur down
from the secular city
to the Eastern Townships

where parish names were English
St. James of Compton
St. Barnabas of Milby

but by then the inhabitants
were mostly Roman Catholic and French
They lived in a large rectory

with a wood-burning stove
clear spring water from Windy Hill
with an occasional newt in it

a hand-cranked telephone on the wall
that worked well except on Sunday mornings
when Mrs. Spaulding the operator was at Mass

and towards evening the sound
of distant cowbells   the cows
coming home by themselves to be milked

My Uncle Arthur rarely drove
I remember one Sunday morning when
in Coaticook for the Eucharist service

he unloaded his black leather bag
with the wafers wine chalice paten
his alb chasuble and stole

from the trunk of their pre-war Plymouth
and laid it on the sand behind the car
Aunt Mary still at the wheel

where she could not see
began to back up
into what was for a few seconds

an impending crisis
of vehicular sacrilege
I remember both

my own secular shout
laced with adrenalin
stop the car, Aunt Mary!

and Uncle Arthur
with his prayerful fingers
his influent smile

fixed on a sphere
I had not yet glimpsed
saying very gently

in that meekness of spirit
that shall inherit the earth
and has changed my life

Marie ... Marie ...

OCCITANIAN SPRING

To Susan Burgess Shenstone

A half-century of silence
and now thanks to a friend's email
I can write to you for the first time

about our bicycle trip together
after that freezing winter in Paris
when my new friend P went insane
and I myself my socialist
faith having foundered
in the intrigues of post-war Europe
between the Communist graffiti
and *chars blindés* in the boulevards   *tanks*
was reading the letters of Van Gogh
waiting as I thought for my own
inevitable madness to kick in

when two Americans proposed a tour
of the churches in southern France
I was ambivalent from guilt
at my many absences from Sciences Po
and you who had just gotten engaged
only joined reluctantly
because Chuck and Lute would be there
as necessary chaperones

We bicycled from Périgueux's
cathedral so restored
a century earlier by Viollet-le-Duc
it looked like a railway station
to the cave of Lascaux
opened just three weeks before
where we all stood in darkness
until the tour-guide lit his match
so that we too could discern
the galloping silent bison
hidden away in this cave
for twenty thousand years

Then our eyes opened
to the art of the Middle Ages
Beaulieu where the angels danced
above the opened coffins of the dead
the basilica at Conques
crammed into a small canyon
we looked across as the dawn sun
came down the opposite hill
through blossoming almond and crocus
to where they opened for us the crypt
of the tenth-century gold virgin
whose stiff imploring arms were
for better or worse encrusted
with Roman cameos and gems

We biked unwittingly down
the same narrow roads where
Eliot and Pound had walked together
only thirty years before us
the wave pattern cut in the stone   *Cantos 29/145*
to Albi's fortress cathedral
austere outside sumptuous within
memorializing the struggle
of the church against the Cathars
in an inscribed world of saints
heretics suppressed cultures
and sublimated adoration
I had never conceived of
in my Protestant corner of Quebec

And then disaster – the missed
rendez-vous at evening
with our chaperones simply gone
us panicked at being alone
and you red-eyed insisting
we must return at once to Paris
but there were no good connections

so we didn't We took a bus
up up to the high bare
causses of the Massif Central
with crags like agonized dolmens
barely sheltering the sheep
and down to the warm paradise
of Lodève and Montpellier
for me at least an entrance
into a new and menacingly
fragrant Mediterranean world

of flamingos landing in the Camargue
the *courses de taureaux*
in the Roman arena at Arles
the ruined abbey at Montmajour
we explored alone at sunset
whose stairwell I descended into darkness
step by step until suddenly
there was nothing more to step on

All my life I have tried
to recover this. Next spring
I at La Pierre Qui Vire   *Burgundian monastery*
walked among jonquils once again
After that with my first wife
I hitch-hiked through the Dordogne
en route to Bosnia
Finally with my second wife
I toured Provence in a rental Lancia
It could not be the same

as that first awkward trip
with fumes of diesel and cherry
over wet tarmac
or crushed thyme on the hillside
and the hot breath of the mistral
in our face as we struggled back north
(towards the broken bridge at Avignon
and the inevitable train station
back to our Canadian lives)
pedaling by the columns
of a restored Roman city
and the very olive groves which
unbeknownst to us
Van Gogh had painted
from the nearby small asylum

When you left I was still
as inhibited as when we began
We never even kissed good-bye
nor did I receive any hint
if your heart had melted
like mine and Bernart's
at the faint falling cadences
of the skylark tumbling overhead
after the sunny rainburst
still heard after decades
of teaching Bernart here out west

B. de Ventadorn

Can vei la lauzeta mover
When I see the skylark beat
With joy its wings against the sun
Till he forgets to fly, and falls
From the sheer sweetness in his heart
Ah! what envy I have then
Of those whom I see rejoicing
I marvel, that from desire
My heart does not melt at once

as I a self-made medievalist
came slowly to realize
I had not been ready at twenty-one
for the deepest mysteries in life
but was blessed to have suffered
intense Petrarcan yearning
with pains I cannot now conceive of
to open my eyes and heart
in that miserable first year
of my supposed adulthood
and disengagement from my private past
I would not now change
for anything in the world.

RENVOI

(from Susan Burgess Shenstone)

We had stopped for a rest
above the side of the road.
with the hills behind us, hills
which had sheep grazing
it was after we had missed the train

and we heard this sweet haunting voice singing
Il y a des moutons blancs
Belle rose du printemps
Nor could we see anyone near us
It just seemed to float down from the hills
as the day was ending.
It was quite magical.

I remember only
that I sang it afterwards for years
on the road by myself –
Belle rose du printemps.

1950, January 2007

WITTENHAM CLUMPS

For Sally Phillips

Whom the gods love die young.
– Titus Maccius Plautus

i

He still cannot believe
that when she was seventeen

she was so beautiful
I mean deeply, inwardly beautiful

he sensed she would soon die.
One day from the Thames-side Manor House

of her mother, Rosamond Lehmann
which was reached on foot

through fields and across a lock
they walked up the Wittenham Clumps

to look at the aged inscription
in the bark of an oak tree

they mistook for a love poem.
A Canadian, he was overwhelmed

by her operatic gentle voice
that had been trained in Milan

even that her father would soon be
the first Communist in the House of Lords.

The day ended
with one rich goodbye kiss on the lock.

It was lucky the country bus
in which he bounced deliriously

all the way back to Oxford
had a roof. Otherwise

his soul perhaps even his body
might have blown away.

ii

When she fell ill with a quinsy
he sent her a comic poem from the New World

with a misremembered epigraph
"Whom the gods love, they take back early"

a joke from his clumsy heart
which for the rest of his life

he wished he could take back
as if he had somehow helped determine

that only six years later
she would die in Indonesia

at the age of twenty-three.

iii

Years later in his middle age
back in Oxford at a lengthy breakfast

he told the story of Sally to his aunt
who believed in spirits and visitations

having, when still fresh from Montreal
brought blackthorn into an Irish manor house

to the dismay of her hostess, who threw it out
saying, "Don't you know it brings death?"

and three weeks later the woman's husband died.
His aunt had told him about the Balliol ghost

and once reduced him, a sceptic, to trembling
as she made him draw, not once but twice in a row

the right card from a full deck,
a feat he never dared again.

Now he told her how Rosamond, distraught
had written a whole book describing

Sally's returns to guide her in this life.
And somehow that same afternoon

somewhere deep in the Cotswolds
having missed a turn

at a badly marked corner three miles back
he and his aunt came to a village

whose triangular common
had a duck pond in it

and where near the graveyard entrance
they were both shocked

incredulous
to discover Sally's grave.

iv

And now very late
Sally came to him yet again

as he an old man in Thailand
meditated on his wife

helping young husbands to locate
their newlywed brides

among the blackened corpses
of the tsunami.

It was almost as if Sally and he
were witnessing together

from up close but also elsewhere
in some other realm

once again the force
of such stopped love, such death.

Thailand, 1/5/05

SOMETHING PRECIOUS

These novels promising
sexual insights and delights
why does something wake me before dawn
and murmur in my own voice *No!*
I do not want to read them?
Am I still at seventy-eight
just being inhibited
or am I like those in our republic
and those others outside our republic
who consider it shameless?

And why do I instantly remember
Geneviève half-blocking the doorway
to her room in the Austrian chalet
with a half-profile stance that somehow
seemed to beckon me in
when I knew nothing about her
except that she had a French title
and was intently sexy? –
As I retreated in confusion
from the voice clamoring *No!*
I was filled with self-loathing
at my failure to be like my friends
a normal Benthamite
pleasure-seeking animal

like the beautiful married woman
who with others nearby
blocked the cellar doorway
kissed me hard on the mouth
and said, *You know I love you* –
what stern voice warned me
this was more than I could handle?
I fled Montreal
to attempt a new life

or years later in Geneva
the British diplomat C
with whom I shared *fondant*
and slightly drunken flirtation
while Maylie was back in Ottawa
pregnant with our first child –
our walk back was so auspicious
I thought that after I left her
at the large door of her room
in the Hôtel du Rhône
she must have been puzzled if not angry
at the uncouthness of this Prufrockian
Strether out of Woollett

or the dyed and acned blonde
who strode into the Canadian pavilion
where I sat in for our Embassy
at the Poznán Trade Fair
and told me what *good times*
she had had the year before
with my predecessor O –
my instantaneous revulsion
had nothing to do with my sense
that she was bait from the UB   *Polish secret police*

or the student in the '60s
who in my office hour
sat on my desk and told me
with her calf grazing my knee
it was wonderful
how the new permissiveness
enabled students and faculty
to become *more intimate* –
by then I was thirty-five
and opening to the erotic
electricity of *a new age*
but a voice still whispered *No!*

or B the writer in Manhattan
on topics we both shared
who ordered in for lunch
three dozen oysters on their shells
and whose urgings to reschedule
my flight home to Berkeley
I eventually declined –

for all this I am now grateful
I have arrived where I am
in a place where it is o.k.
to be (like Eliot and James)
a tad abnormal

It wasn't ever that I was
or was even trying to be virtuous –
between my two marriages
thanks to the stratagem
of a friendly go-between
I lived with someone for years
and was quite at ease
after I had overcome
initial ambivalences of shame

It wasn't at all a matter
of virtue resisting temptation –
at times this was stronger than fear
an involuntary warning
something precious was at stake
something perhaps in the right lobe
a Socratic *daimon*
that might be lost
or even something sacral
unto all generations

or even if it were nothing more
than to do with my dear father
with his nighttime absences *at work*
his two trunks full of love letters
(*Not to be opened until
fifty years after my death*)
and his books not finished –
to me now it would still be precious

I suspect I was   selfishly
protecting in myself
a source akin to what
is celebrated in music
and easily translatable
into so many languages
yet nowhere in the vocabulary
of our left-lobe Western science

âme anima dusza душа
ψυχή soul   *dusha*
                                              psyche

which I recognized
in the Thai woman
who called me her *dtaa* or grandfather –
we talked together for three years
until when we said *Goodbye*
she finally for the first time
hugged me
and her tears fell like pearls

May 2007

HOLY LAND I: TRUTH

"He who sees a need and waits to be asked for help is as unkind as if he had refused it."
– Dante

"Hell is realizing that one did not help when one could have."
– James Mawdsley

I have come to this Holy Land
of limestone and olive trees
with signposts to Armageddon   *Megiddo*
where every salutation –
Shalom! Salaam! – is *Peace!*
but talk is of *we* and *they*
I listen and am obsessed
by how much I dare not say

The young settler on the escarpment
looking down on the Dead Sea
spoke of the vineyard they had planted
and how much she loved the land
Pointing down to the Arab villages
she said one was OK
the other *not so good*
Who will pick your grapes? I asked
and was mute when she said she would

The Tao that can be expressed
is not the true Tao ...   *Tao Te Ching 1*
Can this excuse or explain
my reluctance throughout my life
to meet hate with lovingkindness?

Like those many times in Berkeley
when N boasted of his practice
at the Lake Chabot rifle range
with Black Panthers on his left
John Birchers on his right
all aware they were getting ready
for the day they would shoot each other
What did I ever say?
What was there for me to say?

Useless to give that settler
Auden's anguished dilemma
We must love one another or die
but perhaps I could have appealed
to the faith she was living by
the truth laid out in Torah
if not *Thou shalt love thy neighbor*   *Leviticus 19:18*
at least *do not oppress*
the stranger among you
since *you were strangers* too   *Leviticus 19:33–34*

Our West Coast faiths are mellowed
remote from the hate and blood
exhausted years before
by decades of Holy War
Josephus lays out clearly
how through murder and treason
Jewish Zealots defiled this Mount
till the Romans burned the city

Jewish War IV.286–388,
VI.401–VII.1

For hate to be satisfied
will it be necessary
to endure all this again?

Just as Aeneas's escape
from the walls of burning Troy
is said to have helped refine
his archaic piety
into that of a new city
imposing peace with law
for the haughty to *be brought low*

Aeneid VI.852
Isaiah 2:17, Aeneid VI.853

so Rabbi Yochanan escaped
Jerusalem's holocaust
and developed prayer and study
to replace the burnt-out temple
of animal sacrifice.

Yochanan ben Zakkai
Talmud Gittin:56b
Mishnah

This has been the way of the world
refinement by conflagration
Is there not some other way?

The neglected masses
of Christendom and Islam
from the hillfolk of America
to the hillfolk of Lebanon
confounded by the forces
of merciless intellect
retreat into the solaces
of simplifying sect
And as empires spread again
so Zealots too return

Something hovers over this poem
nudging me to affirm
I have glimpsed *the right path*
where our lives are not deformed
which is why I feel such pain
that I did not express
what Dante had envisioned –
with Empire and church collapsed
in fearful apocalypse   *Purgatorio 32:121–60*
Popes and Emperor in Hell
from selfishness and greed –   *Inf. 10:119, 11:8, 19:44–118*

as a sweet new
different society
with the force of a *gentle heart*   *cor gentil*
able to change the world
I was able to share with my class

No time to grieve for roses
when the forests are burning   *Słowacki*
here in this Holy Land
of Katyushas and M-16s
with the dollar in steep decline
from the war our mellowed movement
was powerless to stop

my memory now half gone
I must look to a stronger voice
with more settled conviction
to narrow the jagged gap
between the truth we are born into
and the truth that has always been
(*for in these things I delight, saith the Lord*)   *Jeremiah 9:24*
in lovingkindness

Jerusalem, 11/13/07

HOLY LAND II: FORCE

La vraie civilisation n'est pas dans le gaz ...
– Marcuse, Eros and Civilization, 153

From some deep instinct roused
by the shock of a kindly man
muttering softly but intently
as we drive from the shell-pocked city
to the mosaic of Orpheus
gently charming the birds

in the ruins of Sephoris   *Zippori*
where Judeo-Christians healed   *Renan History of the Origins V*
the Mishnah was compiled
and until 1948
the Crusader tower
was an Arab school

the Americans should have taken all their planes
and flattened Mecca ...

and the shock of my silence

I am absurdly obsessed
by my gaffe two decades ago
at the radical chic party
for Astorga the Sandinista   *Nora Astorga*
guerrillera and UN ambassador
(with *connections to the powerful*
Somoza family)
by then pale with terminal cancer
but still beautiful

who quit her safe career
as a corporate lawyer
having finally been convinced
that *a rifle*
cannot be met with a flower   *Astorga*

and who professed no guilt
(*He was too much of a monster*)   *Astorga*
when the Somoza general
she had seduced to her apartment
resisted being kidnapped
so her comrades slit his throat.

From some wild impulse
while chatting with Dekka Treuhaft
the Communist whose sister
was Duchess of Devonshire
Dekka who helped bust racist
housing covenants in Berkeley
who gave a little needed
pizzazz to our antiwar movement
and whose son Ben outwitted
the hapless State Department
with his exports to embargoed Cuba
of used pianos

cf. Virgil Georgics 4:488
Jessica Mitford

I was moved to tell Dekka
how in the Cotswold graveyard
below the hilltop church
with the stained-glass windows
naming her titled parents
the very same day
I had revisited Sally's home
I had stumbled incredibly
on Sally's tomb
showing her dead at twenty-three

Sally Philipps Kavanaugh

as if Sally my Rilkean angel
had guided me there herself
the way her mother Rosamond Lehmann
had spoken of her
in her bizarrely spiritualist book
as a *corn goddess Persephone*   *Lehmann, Swan in the Evening 101*
with a sweet returning *force*

at which words – *Rosamond Lehmann* –
Dekka turned away
with a look of what I still
vividly remember
as Communist aristocratic
anticolonial scorn.

We are mysteries to ourselves!
As to why I plagued Dekka
with Rosamond's belief
in Sally as a *revenant*
which was treated solemnly
by a feminist critic   *Shirley Neuman, Genre, Trope, Gender 62*
but by Nancy Mitford not   *Selina Hastings, Rosamond Lehmann*
    354, Guardian 6/8/02

33

I suppose what I really wanted
(assuming it was I)
was to engage her with Dante
who from the refining love
of beauty transfixed in death
wrote of a sweet new
different society
with the force of a *gentle heart*   *cor gentil*
able to change the world

Dante who expounded
what love *dictates within*   *Purgatorio 24:54*
and who dared to name *the cause*   *la cagion*
of what makes the world wicked   *che'l mondo ha fatto reo*
as *bad government*   *mala condotta*
not nature corrupt in us   *Purgatorio 16:103–05*

followed by Hőlderlin
Schiller Marcuse
who all hoped original sin
would prove to be historical
diminished by *civilization*   *Baudelaire; Eliot; Marcuse*

like Wordsworth who after
his faith was nearly broken
by the shock of the guillotine
and years of counterrevolution
claimed he himself could soften
the future – *what we have loved,*
others will love, and we will teach them how   *Prelude 14:446–47*

but facing hunger and massacre
how could one have hoped
to persuade Dekka's rebel
aristocratic heart
with middle-class Canadian
talk of *gentleness*
not to mention *courteous love*?

Amid the *senseless* crowd
Dante's hopes for empire shattered
he wrote in the end it was best
to be a *party for himself*   *cf. Paradiso 17:62, 68–69*
just as Hőlderlin broken-hearted
that the world had denied his freedom
died in an asylum

And now a vivid nightmare
of the counselors at my camp
gone off to some rich hotel
while those bullies long forgotten
cast my belongings about
evincing the violence
that explodes within myself
I awake relieved
to be only where I am
chastised with self-rebuke

The Tao that can be expressed
is not the true Tao ...
How then shall we make use
of the *most incomprehensible*
mystery of the universe –
that as Einstein said
it is comprehensible?

Tao Te Ching 1

Einstein 1935

If the deep structure of our mind
is somehow fitting
to the structure of the cosmos
dare we imagine our instincts
however fallible
could be somehow fitting as well

in the universe emerging
since the axial age   *Jaspers, Way to Wisdom 99–100*
dreamt by meditators
the whole world over
all clinging *tightly*
to the virtue of peace   *Rebbe Nachman of Breslov*

as our hopes whirled
in the conflicts of history
slowly become gentler
just as pebbles tossed
by the tides of the sea
surely become more smooth

to help explain how
in the throes of disaster
hatred violence madness
the world becomes more lovable (as in
the faces of the young women
who brush right by me
on their morning runs)

so that a few maintain
that *all will be well*   *Julian of Norwich, Showings 225*
and others rightly or wrongly
are still willing to risk death
for love to prevail?

Mosaic Orpheus
in the House of the Nile
gently charming the birds
and *calming tigers*   *mulcentem tigris Virgil Georgics 4:510*
with wisdom from having seen
ghosts driven like leaves
in the gusts of a wintry gale

with *great Caesar* once again
on the *Euphrates*   *Virgil Georgics 4:560–61*
I write of a trivial wrong
and bless that kindly man
who helped me recognize
in the light beyond all words
the world can what it can

Haifa, 11/14/07

CONFESSION

For Paul Almond

I saw myself as a humanist
searching the right way to love
our religious species

who became a theist
accepting God's will
that texts be critically examined

and slowly released
from their burdensome and divisive
contexts of external practice

but at last seeing myself
as a child of Jewish observance
and of Buddhist compassion

a small voice inside me
has persuaded me to confess

I am a Christian
seeking to be enlightened

enlightened: not in the sense
of Naipaul's *Beyond Belief*

or the gnosticisms
of Yeats and Pound

but openness to the simple
living waters of the Lord's Prayer   *Song of Songs 4:16*

in the spirit of Merton's
I am a Jew and a Moslem   *Merton, Striving Towards Being 137*

open to other precepts
love the Lord in Hebrew   *Deut 6:5*

love thy neighbor in koine Greek   *Septuagint Leviticus 19:18*
the straight path in Arabic   *Qur'an 1:6*

all things are impermanent   *Mahaparinibbana Sutta 14*
the nameable name is not eternal   *Tao Te Ching 1*

precepts unburdened
by the travails of past Councils

like the priests in *Utopia*
of exceeding holiness

and therefore very few   *More, Utopia 2*

December 2007

II

The Size of Earth

MAE SALONG

After the Thai government granted the KMT refugee status in the 1960s, efforts were made to incorporate the Yunnanese and their families into the Thai nation. Until the late 1980s they didn't have much success, as many ex-KMT were deeply involved in the Golden Triangle opium trade … Because of the rough, mountainous terrain and lack of sealed roads, the outside world was rather cut off from the goings-on in Mae Salong. The KMT never denied its role in drug-trafficking, but justified it by claiming that the money was used to buy weapons to fight the communists.
– Lonely Planet, *Chiang Mai and Northern Thailand*, 247.

The wrinkled woman
splashes tea over the table
rubs the cup with both hands

and savors the fragrant oolong
from bushes in tight neat rows
on the steep ochre hillside below us

a crop substitution program
not like the denuded
Myanmar crags to the west

sleeping in their mist
that not so long ago
were still dense with poppies

The booths across the street
of Akha women in cowries and coins
(their monkey chained to a pole)

line what was once an airstrip
below the monumental
tomb of General Tuan

who profited handsomely
from the opium trade
his son runs the resort   *Lonely Planet 248*

We read the damp-stained captions
about the hundreds who died
in the 1970s campaign

against local insurgents
and we stop for a moment
before the pagoda

in the middle of the courtyard
of this fortress settlement
(*almost an independent state*

until the road was sealed)
out of respect for the dead
Having written to attack

the KMT drug traffickers
and Gen. Kriangsak who in gratitude
for their defense of Thailand

and personal payoffs
of *half a million per year*   *Mills 770*
gave them Thai nationality

and now startled by the photo
of Gen. Tuan with two smiling
bhikkus in saffron robes I wonder   *monks*

Could I have been wrong?
Why shouldn't they be smiling?
the monks here survived

while in Cambodia not far away
they were killed by the thousands
(the bride's story of her aunt

whose throat was cut publicly
for having eaten a raw potato)
by the Khmers Rouges

whom at one point both China
and the US supported
in the days when I myself

from naïve broad-mindedness
quoted from Chairman Mao
The mosque at the center of town

across from the Golden Dragon
reminds me of the grandiose
plans of General Chennault

to contain China from the west
by inciting the Yunnanese Muslims
descended from the armies of Kublai Khan

that lapsed into the lawlessness
of marauding Shan armies
Kachins Karens Was

and I think *not one of us is free*
from this karma of suffering
The cemetery too large

for a mountain-top village
is some miles away
near Mae Sai the city

evacuated just last year
because of cross-border shelling
And yet this nation

where five Buddhist schools
were bombed on Wednesday
disturbs and frightens me less

than the college-educated
planners of preemptive war
back home in the Bush White House

the fighting here was local
the fears human
almost everything that happens here is human

the sow studies the dead piglet
children squat in the once-crowded courtyard
I eat cashew chicken

in the tourist restaurant
that was once an army canteen
and ask our fifteen-year-old waitress

who brings us the bill *Were*
you born here in this village?
and she answers *No*

in China   China?
In this K M T village?
Does this have to do with Islam?

Or with the *tons of heroin*
still exported through Thailand
each year for the last four decades?

> *By not knowing*
> *we enter the way*   Ryokan

as the monkey gestures with its chain

WAT PA NANACHAT

Ajahn Chah … spent … a very brief but significant time with Venerable Ajahn Mun, the most outstanding meditation Master of the ascetic, forest-dwelling tradition. Following his time with Venerable Ajahn Mun, he spent a number of years traveling around Thailand, spending his time in forests and charnel grounds, ideal places for developing meditation practice.

At length he came within the vicinity of the village of his birth, and when word got around that he was in the area, he was invited to set up a monastery at the Pa Pong forest, a place at this time reputed to be the habitat of wild animals and ghosts …

In 1966 the first westerner came to stay at Wat Pa Pong (Wat=temple), Venerable Sumedho Bhikkhu. From that time on, the number of foreign people who came to Ajahn Chah began steadily to increase, until in 1975 the first branch monastery for western and other non-Thai nationals, Wat Pa Nanachat, was set up with Venerable Ajahn Sumedho as abbot.
– Web: <ksc15.th.com/petsei/biography.htm>

leaf forms trembling
in the forest pool of marble

where monks at night
once listened for tiger's breath

we watch a long green snake   *(a python)*
loop itself through the ironwork

then belly-flop – phlat!!
into the dry teak leaves

behind the sun-spattered terra cotta Buddha
impossible for some minutes

to keep eyes closed
to stop listening

for slither

insuperable biases of language
one side talking   *spirits* and *devas*
the other of *superstition*

I only know
that when I come back by *tuk-tuk*   *three-wheeled taxi*
and step through the forest gate

my pace slows
I stop looking

for the purple sunbirds
as I feel breathed into me

something from beyond this
linguistic aporia   *difficulty, straits (Greek)*

around us on all sides
the slow creaking of the tall bamboos

big leaves you can almost hear
when they zigzag down through the butterflies

from the dipterocarpus and strangler figs
in the almost sunless gloom

the darkness of the forest
opening the darkness within us

the wat once walled
inside the forest
as Thailand in Buddhism

and now the forest
or what is left of the forest
walled inside the wat

The Thai student from Cornell
who interviewed elderly monks
about the *thudong* tradition   *ascetic practice*

wrote in her Ph.D. thesis
Between 1950 and 1975
the US provided Thailand

with $650 billion in support
of economic development   *Tiyavanich 368*
dams golf courses and tourist resorts   *Tiyavanich 244*

In the 1960s, nearly 60%
of the country was forested
and now *17%*   *TIMEasia.com*

until *in November 1988*
rain falling on denuded hillsides
killed hundreds of people   *Tiyavanich 245*

logging since then illegal
meaning another source of graft
along with prostitution and drugs   *Pasuk 141–42*

eucalyptus planted
for export to the Japanese
in the midst of the peasants' rice   *Tiyavanich 247*

Her dissertation director
who had approved of this *high rate of growth*
as *a very considerable achievement*   *Wyatt 282–83*

and justified clearing forests
by the *major security crisis*   *Wyatt 290*
in the shadow of Vietnam   *Wyatt 285*

wrote a foreword to her book
everything I knew
had to be thrown away and rethought   *Tiyavanich xi*

he had already written
that Sarit after his coup
arrested *intellectuals and journalists*   *Wyatt 280*

but not how he put Phimontham
the leading meditation monk
into prison for five years

if everyone closed his eyes
how to *watch for communists?*   *Carr 10; Tiyavanich 231*

the wandering monks chastised   *thudong monks*
some of them maybe killed

every kuti was burnt down   *monk's cell*
all the fruit trees around the wat
mango longan lime coconut   *Tiyavanich 234*

while Ajahn Chah
gave up the wandering life
created his own *wat pa*   *forest monastery*

and later Wat Pa Nanachat   *international forest monastery*
Theravadan Buddhism
now in England California
Australia New Zealand Switzerland

insight   the power of caring
as we never knew it in America

the power of Luang Por Ophad   *Venerable Abbot Ophad*
to read our minds
in less than fifteen minutes

saying first to Ronna
after spitting his betel nut
into a bronze spittoon

words I had used that very day
about teaching in Thailand

you can't do one hundred percent
if you can do fifty
do fifty

and then scolding me
You have little bit samadhi   *enlightenment*
but your mind is sokopok   *dirty, defiled*

and too scattered
as if reading my own fears
so as to change my life

this power of insight
was once as widespread
as the transboreal forest

saints like Alcuin and Wang Wei
drawing on its images

to express the wilderness within Scott 525–30
imprinting their holiness

which aged inevitably
into education and science
social development

at the expense of mental development *bhavana*
I learned this as a medievalist

all the dhammas are one *dharmas*
converging

under the glass case
containing the portrait and skeleton
of the young woman who killed herself
when her husband was unfaithful

I sit trying to draw *chi*
up the ladder of my spine

thinking *what have we done to Thailand?*
good roads electricity
no beggars here at the gate

like the children carrying babies
crowding around us in Tachilek
across the border in Myanmar

or the two Cambodian girls at the border
searching each other for lice

or those banging their pans in Varanesi
their legs crushed or amputated
for the sake of charity

if you spend a night
at Tha Ton Riverview resort
you can hear shots over the border

or wake to a corpse
floating down the Mae Kok River

as down the Mekong in Laos
arms battened to a frame of bamboo

part of me thinks

    no question about it
    Thailand has escaped
    the bitter colonial legacies
    of Britain and France
    still leaving their imprint
    of poverty and hatred

but Thailand independent
since the eighteenth century
when Ayudhya was larger than London

remained a forested country
until the 1960s
and the American billions
for *counterinsurgency* and *development*

with villagers displaced
from the new growth eucalyptus
to *become migrant workers*
or prostitutes in Bangkok   *Tiyavanich 245*

even after the insurgency
Phra Prachak discovered
when he ordained the oldest trees
by wrapping them in saffron robes   *River 12*

that what was left of the forest in Dong Yai
remained a battleground   *Tiyavanich 246*

illegal loggers
in league with the military
grenades thrown at his monastery
the roof of his hut
splattered with M16 shots   *Pasanno*

officials petitioning to have him defrocked
till he was finally arrested

now nothing left
but a saffron robe in a kuti   monk's cell
books strewn on the floor
small statues of Buddha in disarray   Bangkok Post 1/4/98

villagers forced out at gunpoint
some of their *crops plowed under*
in other places orderly rows
of another crop planted
in the middle of their rice   Tiyavanich 247

Ajahn Wan: *in today's society*
those who know how to extort
oppress and control others
are regarded as geniuses   Tiyavanich 243

and Ajahn Chah: *if you try to live simply*
practicing the Dhamma
they say you're obstructing progress   Tiyavanich 241

but part of me thinks

        it was happening anyway
        even some Buddhists
        engaged in the crackdown
        Ajahn Uan the sangha head
        looked down on meditation monks
        and *tried to force them out*
        forbidding villagers to give them alms   Tiyavanich 173–75

until he *became so sick*
he had to take food intravenously
and *meditation practice*
helped him gradually recover   *Tiyavanich 194–95*

even then *the Sangha Council*
in 1987
ordered all ascetics to leave the forests   *Tiyavanich 249*

I try to look on it
as an exercise
in letting go
that gladness or sadness
is not the mind
only a mood
coming to deceive us   *Chah 1*

caring   *teach us*
to care and not to care

great fame in the end
for Luang Por Chah

people came by busloads
they say they're looking for merit
but they don't give up vice   *Tiyavanich 289*

Ajahn Chah *often said*
he felt like a monkey on a string
when I get tired
maybe they throw me a banana   *Tiyavanich 292*

the cuckoo-like bird
sings gaily *Moha*
Moha   the death of the dharma

in the withered sun-loud glade

BIBLIOGRAPHY

Stephen Carr, "An Ambassador of Buddhism to the West," in *Buddhism
    in Europe*, edited by Aad Verboom (Bangkok: Crem. Vol. Somdet Phra
    Phuttajan, Wat Mahathat, 1990).
Venerable Ajahn Chah, *A Taste of Freedom* (Bangkok: Liberty Press, 1994).
James Mills, *Underground Empire: Where Crime and Governments Embrace*
    (New York: Dell, 1987).
Ajahn Pasanno, "Saving Forests So There Can Be Forest Monks," *Forest
    Sangha Newsletter*, January 1996, www.abm.ndirect.co.uk/fsn/35/.
Pasuk Phongpaichit, Sungsidh Piriyarangsan, and Nualnoi Treerat, *Guns,
    Girls, Gambling, Ganja: Thailand's Illegal Economy and Public Policy*
    (Chiang Mai: Silkworm Books, 1998).
Jess River, "We must learn to be leaves." *Earth Island Journal* (Fall 1993), 12,
    sino-sv3.sino.uni-heidelberg.de/ FULLTEXT/JR-ADM/river.htm.
P.D. Scott, "Alcuin's *Versus de Cuculo*: The Vision of Pastoral Friendship,"
    Studies in Philology 62, 4 (July 1965), 510–30.

TIMEasia.com. Accessed 21 August 2002.

Kamala Tiyavanich, *Forest Recollections: Wandering Monks in Twentieth-century Thailand* (Chiang Mai: Silkworm Books, 1997).

David K. Wyatt, *Thailand: A Short History* (Chiang Mai: Silkworm Books, 1993).

THE TAO OF 9/11

At the First Emperor's Tomb
the Chinese People's Republic
shows you a preliminary movie
in which this monument of empire

is seen through the eyes of peasants
who rose up in rebellion
and smashed the terra cotta statues
we have come so far to see.

I tried asking whether the government
is more in favor of the tomb
or of its being smashed? The guide answered
Both! We think the tao of history

contains both the bright yang of order
and the dark yin of revolt.
So I said, *Would that mean*
that in history right now

the yin is the Falun Gong?
A short silence. Then
You must understand that in China
there are some things we do not think about.

I know why I'm remembering this.
There are things we don't think about in America
things I don't want to think about myself
like this flood of emails from Russians

whom I have never met
about Far West Ltd.
a meta-group almost unknown
and yet so powerful

it is said to manipulate states
for the ends of the drug traffic
spreading violence in an organized route
from Afghanistan and Kosovo to New York   *Scott '05*

a group which brought its partners –
a Venezuelan close to FARC   *Colombian Revolutionary Armed Forces*
an Israeli advising Thaçi   *chief KLA commander*
and a Turk close to al-Qaeda

to meet in the villa of Khashoggi
once *the richest man in the world*   *Kessler 12*
whom the Senate BCCI Report listed
among *the principal agents of the U.S.*   *Kerry-Brown Report 299*

and arms seller *to the Medellin Cartel*   *DIA Report*
with Voloshin (Berezovsky's man
under Yeltsin in the Kremlin)
and one of the Chechen Basaevs

who then blew up Moscow buildings
as described by John Dunlop   *Dunlop*
shortly after the U.S. and the KLA   *Kosovo Liberation Army*
took over Kosovo   *Scott '05*

Dunlop is reputable
Why did he present the meeting
as a mere plan for a Russian 9/11
at the behest of Yeltsin's Kremlin   *Dunlop*

ignoring the role at the villa
of men like Sosnaliev and Tsveiba
from Abkhazia which now *has become
a key heroin transiting point?*   *Sida/Cornell Caspian '02*

Why did he suppress what his source
said about Surikov and Fritz Ermarth
the Turk and the CIA
the Israeli and the KLA?

Was it because just like myself
he did not want to think
about who was involved in opening
the new Kosovo drug route

after the mad dash of Russian troops
one month before the meeting   *June 11, 1999*
to seize the Pristina airport in Kosovo   *Judah 279, 284–85*
without (it is said) the knowledge of Yeltsin   *Shevtsova 285, fn. 11*

just as Al McCoy and myself
both promptly forgot about the vet
who refused to talk to us
after they firebombed his Jag   *McCoy xii, Scott '89 147–48,*
                                                        Scott '04 38–40

not wanting to face what it means
that you can sell drugs in a DEA sting
and still be released when you tell them
you are *a CIA informant.*   Scott '92 129; Levine 35–36

Two kinds of businesses:
those which flourish from peace
and the strengthening of law
and those which require the opposite

zones of incessant chaos
like Chechnya Colombia Afghanistan
where drugs can be grown or trafficked
under the watch of PMCs.   *private military companies*

The CIA knew what it was doing
when in 2001
they brought back *"Mr. Ten Percent"*   *Haji Mohammed Zaman*
at the top of the heroin trade

from Dijon to Jalalabad   *Smucker 9*
and arranged for the release
of Haji Ayub Afridi from prison   *Raman*
(the same men who in the '80s

had organized *the heroin trail*
to the Soviet troops
i.e. to the clique who became Far West
with the blessings of the CIA)   *Raman*

thus restoring the Afghan
opium economy
after two years of prohibition
under the Taliban.   *Scott '03 33, 43–44*

and pushing America and Russia
still further down the path
of increasing superwealth
and declining average income

(my starting salary in '61   *$7250.00*
could buy a third of a good Berkeley house
as opposed to a twentieth
from a starting salary today)

increasing income disparities
the sign our state is declining
the homeless we no longer support
and have grown used to not thinking about

as we step across them
towards our ATMs
what Sallust and Arnold discerned
in Rome and Victorian London

privatim opulentia
publice egestas   *Sallust, Arnold*
until the republic is suborned
by these forces we cannot see

for which the intellectual price
is a shrinkage of our culture
towards the trivialities
of narcotic distractions undecipherable poets

and expansion of empire
with help from al Qaeda
until now there are American troops
from Kyrgyzstan to Kosovo.

Starting in 1998
Surikov, the Venezuelan, and the Turk
had their own company Far West   *http://www.pravda.info/*
connected with *the secured transport*   *news/2695.html*

of commercial shipments from Afghanistan   *Filin '05*
and with *representatives in the Emirates,*
Afghanistan, Colombia, Kosovo   *http://www.pravda.info/*
and said to have *smuggled to Iran and China*   *news/2695.html*

nuclear-capable missiles
that could strike targets
1,860 miles away   *Naím 279; NBC 3/18/05*
in conjunction with KBR and Alfa-Bank

motivated by profit
wrote the editor of *Foreign Policy*   *Naím 279–80*
but according to Russian sources
the mastermind was Cheney

whose *objective was to create*
a casus belli *against Iran*   *Novyi Region 11/29/06*
under the control of Diligence   *burtsev.ru*
a firm with *success in securing contracts*

from *Neil Bush, the President's brother*   *Financial Times, 12/11/03*
headed by Joe Allbaugh   *Financial Times, 12/11/03; Asia Times, 5/20/04*
who in 2000 organized
both the Bush-Cheney campaign

and the *"19th floor riot"* that
stopped the recount in Miami-Dade County   *Floridagate*
and then was made head of FEMA
the agency that with Cheney and Rumsfeld   *Mann 139; Bamford 72*

had developed "REAGAN'S SECRET COUP PLANS"
in the 1980s   *Progressive Review*
the plans for COG   *Continuity of Government*
the *plans for an anti-constitutional takeover*

in a time of crisis   *Smith, June '98. Cf. New York Times, 11/18/91*
which were implemented on 9/11   *9/11 Report 38; Bamford 66*
with Cheney's two orders – the first
one still unexplained

ten minutes before Flight 77
is supposed to have hit the Pentagon   *Griffin 219–23*
and then a shoot-down order
before the President's plane took off   *Clarke 8*

Both after Bush had entrusted
Cheney, FEMA, and Allbaugh
to set up a terrorism task force
to deal with terrorist attacks   *Houston Chronicle, 5/9/01;*
                                                           Ruppert 412–18

which is said to have changed the rules
making it far more complicated
to deal with hijacked planes   *9/11 Report, 17; cf. fn. 101, 458*
just weeks before 9/11   *Ruppert 412–18*

Far West's leader Vladimir Filin
the suspected chief narcobaron   *Kaledin '03*
confirmed that "a well-known American corporation
is a co-founder of our agency"   *Filin '05*

and after I quoted this
it was reported that Filin cleared
the Pristina dash in advance
with Thaçi and Haradinaj   *Surikov 2006*

described by the London *Observer*
as a drug-trafficker and *the key
US intelligence asset in Kosovo*   *Observer, 9/10/00*
who is now on trial at the Hague   *London Times, 3/8/05*

while Filin and Far West
worked on the Georgian project,
financed by KBR Halliburton, apparently
with the approval of CIA)   *Yasenev*

69

It is too much. I think of Petrov
blown up in his car in Cape Town
after taping his quarrel with Surikov
at the Hotel Bristol in Vienna   *Petrov '04*

and I think of Indira Singh
who lost her job at J.P. Morgan
after she notified the FBI
about Ptech the hi-tech Islamist firm

with contracts at FAA
the White House the Secret Service
and links to the local Al Kifah   *al Qaeda support group*
Singh spoke publicly about Ptech   *NPR Radio, 12/8/02*

when I ran into the drugs
I was told that if I mentioned
the money to the drugs around 9/11
that would be the end of me.   *Indira Singh testimony*

So much to wonder about
so much to be grateful for!
the enormity of the suppressed
should not let us forget the obvious

like Havel's gratitude to Congress
for the liberation of eastern Europe
which Noam found *silly and repugnant*   *Cockburn 149–51*
not having lived there himself

Like the times in a bad marriage
good times flash back with pain
so in the midst of preemptive war
I remember loving this country

that even the CIA
helped Milosz start life anew
back when defectors were still
being *kidnapped in the streets.*   *Illg 17*

But as for 9/11 and drugs
the 9/11 Report denied the connection   *9/11 Report 171*
ignoring the drug money for Ramzi Yousef
from an I.S.I. agent in the Philippines

for a plot covered up
according to an Embassy security official
by *high-ranking officers*
of the CIA and Secret Service   *Alexander Cockburn, Ressa 33*

or the speech by Bonner of Customs
on *the Jafar organization out of Detroit*   *Bonner; cf. Farah 171–72*
(*shipping hash and heroin to the United States*
for almost half a century)   *Goddard and Coleman 24*

Khalid Jafar's bag (said NBC)
was placed on Pan Am 103
without passing through inspection
as *part of a DEA undercover operation*   *Guardian, 11/1/90*

I remember the defeat and fear
in the face of Allan Francovich
the last time he contacted me
via a cut-out   a mutual friend

one year before Allan dropped dead
while going through U.S. Customs   *Independent, 4/28/97*
whose film on Pan Am 103 and Jafar
could be shown in Britain but not this country   *Ganser 49*

though he has since been posthumously vindicated
by *a police chief's signed statement*
that key evidence in the Lockerbie trial
was planted by the CIA;   *Scotsman, 8/28/05*

and what happened to Danny Casolaro   *Goddard and Coleman 352–55*
on the trail of the so-called Octopus   *Beaty and Gwynne 224–25*
until he was "suicided" in West Virginia   *Buffalo News, 8/27/93*
with my name and number in his notebook.

And should I now be trusting V   *2006*
this Russian whose reports on Far West
are corroborated only by Filin's admission
that he himself went to Kosovo?   *Surikov '06*

It is hard to know whom to trust
as I learned back East at a Center   *International Center for*
researching for Senator Kerry's investigation   *Development Policy*
into Contra support operations and drugs.

I think of the secret memo in two copies
I had my secretary a student volunteer
hand-deliver from the Center
to Brian Barger and Bob Parry   *cf. Terrell 297–324; Parry 15*

who phoned back furious
(*Don't write these things down in Washington!*)
and somehow Secord's lawyer got it   *Richard Secord*
to file as a Court Exhibit in the Christic case

and what about Jack Terrell at the Center
a man intimate with the mercenary "community"   *Nation, 8/15/87*
who knew about the military coup in Fiji   *Nation, 8/15/87*
that night before anyone in the press.

Jack was shown to have told the truth
about the Contra cocaine operation
disguised by imports of frozen fish   *Kerry Report, 438; Scott and*
in the memo prepared for Senator Kerry   *Marshall 131*

which was stolen for the Reagan Justice Department   *Scott and*
after which Oliver North   *Marshall 142–43, 148–51;*
called Terrell a "Terrorist Threat"   *Terrell 384, 463;*
and our Center was put under FBI surveillance.   *cf. Kerry*
                                                         Report, 163

So later when Jack said he wanted
to bring his wife to the United States
I (knowing his childhood story
of how when fourteen he had stolen a car

and on the instruction of his father
was sentenced to 18 years in an adult prison)   *Scott and Marshall 127*
gave him the money he needed
for return airfare to Manila

after which a call came from the Center:
Why did you finance Terrell's scheme
to destroy Manglapus (who had been expected   *Philippine Foreign*
to succeed Cory in the Philippines)?   *Secretary; Aquino, cf. Time,*
10/28/91, Terrell 424–32

In this way my naïve good will
implicated me in the defeat
of the one candidate committed to removing
the U.S. military bases.

Still later Jack invited me
to think he might have been the "Carson"
who tricked Bill Pepper with the lie
discrediting his book on Martin Luther King   *Pepper 368, 426–30*

so that we still do not know for certain
who was behind King's murder
any more than about the Kennedys'
or who Jack was really working for

though he claimed that he was told by phone
to penetrate North's Contra support effort
by *Donald Fortier and the* NSC.   *National Security Council,*
Oh Jack! Though I knew enough   *Terrell 38*

never completely to trust you
I still thought of you as my friend   *cf. Terrell 455–60*
and that like me you were fighting drug traffickers
not just that upstart Oliver North.

The American dilemma: to heal this world
we must become intimate with it
but the search for political truth
will lead one deeper and deeper into falsehood

so we all end up like the good Germans
not thinking about who caused the Reichstag Fire
or the hundreds of people we do not know
taken off to secret camps or distant countries.

It is a dilemma: part of me
needs to agree with the left
that we have to wake up America
that knowledge will make us free

the idea being that truth
unites us in thinking together
even though these truths of darkness
have been known to destroy

those who have published them   *Gary Webb, Independent, 10/8/05*
and I myself can share with no one
except those who like myself
have become distanced from the crowd

so that I hate to go on
transmitting the testimony
of witnesses like Steve Carr
who predicted correctly they would be murdered   *Scott and*
Marshall 155; Scott '05

and it is a struggle to keep in mind
that by seeking the truth
from *the hidden sphere of life*
in its hidden openness   *Havel 57; Schell 197*

I have not in fact been alone:
there have always been strangers
some in scattered parts of this land
or in countries unvisited

others though the great chain
of the centuries
who without ever meeting
it is possible to trust

in the truth of *yin*
that is always gentle
like water flowing
to the lowest places   *Tao Te Ching viii*

the Tao where *the soft and gentle*
overcome the hard and strong   *Tao Te Ching xxxvi*
because *truth being that which is*
can never be destroyed   *Gandhi 2:389; Schell 206*

and reminds us that America
the land of nonviolence and violence
snake handlers peace workers baseball movies
sweat lodges genealogists and stock car races

is undefinable
from the jazz of Ledbelly
and concerts of the Grateful Dead
to the Wiffenpoof song

from Whitman's hopes for the unwritten
to the *New Yorker* poets
with a toad in their lawn mower
or snake in their burning brush pile

the land which Reiko aged eighteen
refused to leave
when her parents returned
to tradition-bound Japan.

Uncertain as always
whether this republic is past saving
or whether some of us still tread
the perilous path of the future

part of me just meditates
on the new and more flourishing wildlife
that is improving Point Reyes
ten years after the Mount Vision fire.   *San Francisco Chronicle,*

10/2/05

From the glories of the Tang Dynasty
I recall only one date: the year
the usurper An Lushan
drove both Wang Wei and Du Fu

far from the corrupt court
into the mountains
where for the first time they were free
to write the only poems we remember.

BIBLIOGRAPHY

Matthew Arnold, *Culture and Anarchy*, http://www.authorama.com/culture-and-anarchy-3.html.

James Bamford, *A Pretext for War: 9/11, Iraq, and the Abuse of America's Intelligence Agencies* (New York: Doubleday, 2004).

Jonathan Beaty and S.C. Gwynne, *The Outlaw Bank: A Wild Ride into the Secret Heart of BCCI* (New York: Random House, 1993).

Robert Bonner (Customs), DEA Press Release, January 10, 2002, http://www.usdoj.gov.dea/major/me3.html.

Burtsev.ru, "US Companies Linked to Vice-President Cheney Supervised the Transfer of Ukrainian WMD to Iran," http://left.ru/burtsev/ops/novyiregion.phtml.

Richard A. Clarke, *Against All Enemies: Inside America's War on Terrorism* (New York: Simon & Schuster, 2004).

Alexander Cockburn, *The Golden Age Is In Us* (London: Verso, 1995).

DIA Report of 9/23/91, "Subj: (U) IIR [DELETED]/Narcotics – Colombian Narco-Trafficker Profiles," http://www.gwu.edu/~nsarchiv/NSAEBB/NSAEBB131/dia910923.pdf.

John B. Dunlop, "'Storm in Moscow': A Plan of the Yeltsin "Family" to Destabilize Russia," The Hoover Institution, October 8, 2004, http://www.sais.jhu.edu/programs/res/papers/Dunlop%20paper.pdf.

Douglas Farah, *Blood from Stones: The Secret Financial Network of Terror* (New York: Broadway Books, 2004).

Filin Interview, *Pravda-Info*, September 2, 2005, http://www.pravda.info/region/3601.html.

"Floridagate, or 'Hey, what's 2.5 million votes between friends?'" http://www.geocities.com/goretothecore/floridagate/.

Mohandas K. Gandhi, *Selected Works*, ed. Narayan (Ahmedabad: Najivan Publishing Hoise, 1968).

Daniele Ganser, *Operation Gladio: NATO's Top Secret Stay-Behind Armies and Terrorism in Western Europe* (London: Frank Cass Publishers, 2005).

Donald Goddard with Lester K. Coleman, *Trail of the Octopus: From Beirut to Lockerbie – inside the DIA* (London: Bloomsbury, 1993).

David Ray Griffin, *The 9/11 Commission Report: Omissions and Distortions* (Northampton, MA: Olive Branch Press/Interlink, 2004).

Václav Havel, *Living in Truth* (London: Faber & Faber, 1986).

Jerzy Illg, "An Invisible Rope: Czesław Miłosz in the Literary Underground in Poland," *Periphery,* Vol. 4/5, 1999, http://www-personal.engin.umich.edu/~zbigniew/Periphery/No4/illg.html.

Tim Judah, *Kosovo: War and Revenge* (New Haven: Yale University Press, 2002), 279, 284–85.

Nikita Kaledin, "Героиновый тур," Stringer-news, November 4, 2003: http://www.stringer-news.ru/Publication.mhtml?PubID=2448&Part=39.

Kerry Report: U.S. Congress. Senate. Committee on Foreign Relations. Subcommittee on Terrorism, Narcotics, and International Operations. *Drugs, Law Enforcement, and Foreign Policy.* Washington, D.C.: Government Printing Office, 1989.

Kerry-Brown Report: U.S. Congress. Senate, 102nd Cong., 2nd Sess. *The BCCI Affair: A Report to the Senate Committee on Foreign Relations from Senator*

John Kerry, Chairman, and from Senator Hank Brown, Ranking Member,
Subcommittee on Terrorism, Narcotics, and International Operations.

Ronald Kessler, *The Richest Man in the World* (New York: Warner Books,
1986).

Mike Levine, *The Big White Lie* (New York: Thunder's Mouth Press, 1993).

James Mann, *The Rise of the Vulcans: The History of Bush's War Cabinet* (New
York: Viking, 2004).

Alfred W. McCoy, *The Politics of Heroin: CIA Complicity in the Global Drug
Traffic* (Chicago: Lawrence Hill Books/ Chicago Review Press, 2003).

*The 9/11 Commission Report: Final Report of the National Commission on
Terrorist Attacks on the United States*, Authorized Edition (New York:
W.W. Norton, 2004).

NPR Weekend, All Things Considered, December 8, 2002.

Naím, Moisés. *Illicit: How Smugglers, Traffickers, and Copycats Are Hijacking
the Global Economy.* New York: Anchor, 2006.

Novyi Region, 11/29/06, "Кто и как «помог» Украине поставить
стратегические ракеты в Иран?" http://www.nr2.ru/
dnepropetrovsk/94036.html.

Robert Parry, *Secrecy & Privilege: Rise of the Bush Dynasty from Watergate to
Iraq* (Arlington, VA: Media Consortium, 2004).

William F. Pepper, *Orders to Kill: The Truth Behind the Murder of Martin
Luther King* (New York: Carroll and Graf, 1995).

Petrov Audio Recordings, http://www.compromat.ru/main/
surikov/narko.htm.

Pravda-Info, May 3, 2005, "Анатолий Баранов и Антон Суриков вошли в
состав руководства агентства «Far West Ltd»,"
http://www.pravda.info/news/2695.html.

Progressive Review, "The Ronald Reagan Myth,"
http://prorev.com/reagan.htm

B. Raman, "Assassination of Haji Abdul Qadeer in Kabul," South Asia
Analysis Group, Paper No. 489, http://www.saag.org/papers5/
paper489.html.

Maria A. Ressa, *Seeds of Terror: An Eyewitness Account of Al-Qaeda's Newest
Center of Operations in Southeast Asia* (New York: Free Press, 2003).

Michael C. Ruppert, *Crossing the Rubicon: The Decline of the American Empire at the End of the Age of Oil* (Gabriola Island, BC: New Society Publishers, 2004).

Sallust, *Bellum Catilinae*, http://ancienttexts.org/library/latinlibrary/sall.1.html.

Jonathan Schell, *The Unconquerable World: Power, Nonviolence, and the Will of the People* (NewYork: Metropolitan Books/Henry Holt, 2003).

Peter Dale Scott, *Coming to Jakarta* (New York: New Directions, 1989).

Peter Dale Scott, "How the U.S. Government Has Augmented America's Drug Crisis," in Alfred W. McCoy and Alan A. Block, *War on Drugs: Studies in the Failure of U.S. Narcotics Programs*, (Boulder, CO: Westview Press, 1992), 125–77.

Peter Dale Scott, *Drugs, Oil, and War* (Lanham, MD: Rowman & Littlefield, 2003).

Peter Dale Scott, "The Sleep of Reason: Denial, Memory-Work, and the Reconstruction of Social Order," *Literary Responses to Mass Violence* (Waltham, MA: Brandeis University, 2004), 35–43.

Peter Dale Scott, "The Global Drug Meta-Group: Drugs, Managed Violence, and the Russian 9/11," *Lobster*, 10/29/05, http://lobster-magazine.co.uk/articles/global-drug.htm.

Peter Dale Scott, *The Road to 9/11: Wealth, Empire, and the Future of America* (Berkeley and Los Angeles: University of California Press, 2007).

Peter Dale Scott and Jonathan Marshall, *Cocaine Politics: The CIA, Drugs, and Armies in Central America* (Berkeley and Los Angeles: University of California Press, 1991).

Lilia Shevtsova, translated by Antonina Bouis, *Putin's Russia* (Washington: Carnegie Endowment for International Peace, 2003).

SIDA/Cornell Caspian Consulting, "The South Caucasus: A Regional Overview," 2002, http://www.cornellcaspian.com/sida/sida-cfl-2.html.

Indira Singh testimony, 9/11 Citizen's Commission, 130, http://justicefor911.org/September-Hearings.doc.

Sam Smith, "Mind Wars: 'X-Files' Gets It Right," *Progressive Review*, June 1998

Philip Smucker, *Al Qaeda's Great Escape: The Military and the Media on Terror's Trail* (Washington: Brassey's, 2004).

Anton Surikov, *Crime in Russia: The International Implications* (London: Brassey's for the Centre for Defence Studies, University of London, 1995).

Anton Surikov, "The Government of the United States Is Seriously Concerned about the Safety of CIA Analyst," 2006, http://forum.msk.ru/material/power/7495.html.

Jack Terrell with Ron Martz, *Disposable Patriot: Revelations of a Soldier in America's Secret Wars* (Washington: National Press Books, Inc., 1992).

Yuri Yasenev, "Россию ждет оранжевая революция" ("An Orange Revolution is in Store for Russia"), compromat.ru, 12/17/04, http://www.compromat.ru/main/surikov/saidov.htm.

October 2006

MAKING HISTORY, UNFOLDING WORLD

The question is why
to a seminar of senior citizens
mostly younger than myself

I narrated as comedy
my thoughts on the first ever
assault from the air

on a U.S. city – Berkeley
attacked in 1969
by an Army helicopter

dropping CS gas   *incapacitant spray*
over Lower Sproul Plaza   *New York Times, 5/21/69*
which all of us protesting

the occupation of People's Park
by the National Guard
had been told was the only place

where a rally would be permitted
I did not attend
but had a good view from the Wheeler Hall steps

as the helicopter came in low
over the Student Union building
and dropped its white cargo

just as I had already seen
one year earlier
on the front page of the *New York Times*

except that those hippies
fleeing in all directions
from the helicopter's path

were actually soldiers
dressed up for a rehearsal
on a U.S. Army base.

This day I was well positioned
to watch the white cloudlet float away
as the breeze through the Golden Gate

blew it sideways up the hill
to where scholars in the Library
patients in the U.C. hospital

and rich folks up on Grizzly Peak
were incapacitated.

The question is why
I recalled this as a tale
of endearing inefficiency

completely ignoring the perspective
of those trapped in the Plaza
how *lawmen and Guardsmen*

pitched tear gas into the crowd
and with the threat of their bayonets
prevented demonstrators from getting out   Rolling Stone, 6/14/69

(just as in Mexico
at the Tlatelolco massacre
only eight months earlier   Oct. 2, 1968

officers in civilian clothes
were to prevent the entrance
or exit of anyone to the plaza)   Proceso, 10/1/06

as well as the earlier rally
when *shots fired by Sheriff's deputies*
killed bystander James Rector

and wounded about 75 others   San Francisco Chronicle, 4/20/99
in the streets outside Cody's Books
while the next invocation of martial law

under OPERATION GARDEN PLOT   *Covert Action Quarterly,*
left four students dead at Kent State   *Spr-Su 2000*
and completely ignoring the hopeful

teenage girls hanging flowers
on the Guardsmen's bayonets
along the nonviolent march

(which Dohrn of the Weathermen
urged vainly to convert
into a bloody confrontation)

to the stretch of Dwight Way
turfed over by John Reed
where we danced barefoot all afternoon

while Lauren writhed half-naked
on a flatbed truck
in front of the wide-eyed youngsters

from the Central Valley
rigidly "at ease" with their guns
inside Peoples' Park.

Perhaps I lapsed into comedy
as the best way to compose the past
from unconscious conviction

that history's deepest pattern
is not the sickness but the healing
a Pascalian wager

like Dante's and Milton's
that to live in hope
we must let go of our torments.

Or it could have been cowardice
my reluctance to accept
how unlikely were the chances

of any successful healing
in this hatred-nursing nation
mired in fear and debt.

Or it could have been denial
from a repressed sense of guilt
of having by my enthusiastic

opposition to nightsticks and tear gas
helped create the death scene
where a young man was killed.

Or it could have just been biology
my dispassion over the helicopter
(which had once aroused in me

an embarrassing urge to shoot it down)
deriving less from wisdom
than from loss of testosterone.

Or perhaps it was from all of these
the recognition of past
shortcomings on everyone's part

yielding in the end
a little forgiveness and humility –
the right relation

to help time unfold.

THE SIZE OF EARTH:
A SHORT SIMPLE POEM TO GET US OUT OF IRAQ

For Laura and George W. Bush

Having just seen Orion upside down
over Sydney Harbor

my head aligned with the point
of his hanging dagger

my feet with its haft
I gather this stuff we stand on

has two sides

and that from the absence
of parallactic shift

our earth compared to the space
in Orion's dagger

is a speck

almost nothing at all

ii

And that from either edge
of this speck of planet dust

we can look beyond the apparencies
of Northern and Southern Cross

to the great stream of the Milky Way
either upside or down

and the cloudy imaginative source
you shall love   *Deut 10:12*

over and beyond Homer
the Vedas the Da Xue

Dante the Shahnama Marx the Ring
even our epiphanies

and our devotions
leading to massacres

and autos-da-fe

iii

*– literally billions
of planets in our galaxy –*   *New York Times, 10/5/06*

in light of so much unseen
what can we still be sure of?

iv

When we consider ourselves strong
we have the power to create

a hell we cannot think is God's

and when we see we are a speck
each of us a speck on a speck

then we can wake to the glory

v

– consider our withdrawal from Vietnam
– now a tourist destination! –

– not the end of the world

III

Global Sonnets

ABOVE SIBERIA

My plane, after three dull weeks of planning, packing,
Diverted north by an unforeseen typhoon,
Surprises me with this view of Siberian taiga!
Exhilarated, as in youth, by the unexpected –
Alaskan glaciers, the rippled Bering Strait –
I forget my bored obsession with Iraq,
Much as Lowell, in this book slipped from my lap,
Had also to escape America.   *Mariani 384*

Ronna will break her fast in her Thailand *wat*   *monastery*
As the black of night on this electronic map
Edges across my children back in Berkeley.
What is life? This unpredictable, this surprise
That liberates us, Hakkodate, Khabarovsk.
I'm seventy-four. Anything can happen.

9/22/03

ON NOT RECOGNIZING RONNA IN BANGKOK

And even if, after two months separation,
I failed to recognize you at the first
As you walked blinking through the hotel lobby,
It was not, as I said, because you had lost weight,
My Jewish princess, now up before dawn
For one lean meal a day. No! It was your hair,
No longer deeply hennaed round your neck
But drawn back in a knot, and partly gray.

More beautiful to me, now we are both
Graying together, you no longer needing
To imitate the fashion of your youth.
Most beautiful to me, because of this wedded look
In your blurred, radiant eyes, made new again
From your Rains Retreat which I could never share.   *three-month*

retreat

9/23/03

VIEW FROM PHAYAO RAM

From this suite in Phayao's hospital, I look down
On the four-lane highway to Tachilek, and Burma's
Old heroin labs. Queues of motorcycles
Race north and south. To the west are fields, chickens,
Palm trees, bananas, too many dogs. The town
Comes next, white buildings, water towers
Along the lake, above which towering clouds
Stroke the majestic glory of Doi Luang.   *Great Mountain*

A few yards north, a wooden palace serves
The town's best noodles. I ask, "How could noodles
Ever pay for this palace?" I'm told, "The owners
Live here, but cannot sell it. It's been confiscated,
Because of drugs." A sensible, smiling people.
To the east, ten years ago, Thai armies killed each other.

10/1/03

TO CAROL SHIELDS
(whom I never knew)

Ten years late, when emptying my office,
I found your unopened note asking to meet.
It joined the great pile of things to answer
Then burned in the fire, and besides, you now are dead.
But suddenly, at 4 A M last night,
I had to write you from Phayao in Thailand,
Stone Diaries in my hand, and Daisy Flett
Filling my mind as once she must have yours,

Unnursed at birth, changing her lives like clothes
When crossing borders, not knowing what she wanted,
A middler always, waiting to hear *I love you*,
And afraid *to look inside*, to the nothingness   *Shields 356*
Buddhists try to get to. But Thais would say   *Shields 356*
There are worse fates than just to *let life happen*.   *Shields 356*

10/02/03

A half century gone, you are back from Paris
To your Berkeley house, and you begin to cry.
Too many memories, too many deaths. Even
Going into Long's drug store is difficult.
I see Pediolyte on the shelf, and I think,
If only we'd given my niece the drink ourselves
And not taken her to Emergency, where the intern,
Overworked, left the fatal warning in his pocket …

I have since changed pharmacy. And your life.
Mexico, the Swedish baron, opportunities
You chose to let slip away, *governed* (your word)
By fears of inadequacy. I want you to write this story
But you *really want to write about death. Since my whole*
Family is dead, that might be a way to begin.

10/03/03

FOR RAQUEL SCHERR (2)

But you were grieving before the deaths began.
Your easy identity was with your beauty,
Still there, though once *When I walk down a road*
Cars no longer crash into a pole, you told me.
About your intellect you were split in two.
Jewish like your distant father, you doubted
Aztec blood could ever make an achiever,
So were hesitant, then brilliant, then exhausted.

In Sweden you started a new life, your friends
Famous, a career, all seemed inauthentic.
Back home with Lenny, his daily writing gave you
A near-breakdown, anti-depressants, back to teaching,
Less important to do something exceptional
Than anything that would get me up in the morning again.

10/05/03

HOME

Home? I left Canada by accident
Four decades ago, drawn by sheer novelty
And climate. Then stayed, as America fell
To a foolish and unstoppable war.
After my state elected movie stars
I went to Toronto, spent time with new friends
Nearly all of them border-crossers
Who had fled the land where I'm still an alien.

Home is family, friends: six months in Phayao
Then six in Berkeley, not a hellish place
Nor a place I can stay for long, where my granddaughter,
Having heard I was leaving, would not talk to me,
But dug furiously by herself on the silent beach.
"What's this?" "I'm building a bridge, from here to Thailand."

10/07/03; 11/20/03

JACQUES DE COUTRE (1595)

The king pampered his elephants. *They had silk cushions*
On which they slept like puppies, and *six gold basins*:
For oil, water, *food, drink, and needs of nature.*
They were *so well trained that*, when necessary,
They got up from their cushions, the mahouts understood,
And passed them their basins. The day one died,
The king was wracked with grief, four priests stood around it,
For eight days *everyone worshipped on their knees.*

And when a little girl aged eight, who was serving the queen,
Stole a small piece of gold, she and 27 friends
Who had not denounced her, each *had one of their eyes*
        removed,
The skin from their hands detached, their nails torn out
Their flesh stuffed in their mouths. So they should suffer slowly,
They were roasted over a low fire, each in her pan,
        until they died.   *Van der Cruysse 27–31*

10/09/03

WALKING MEDITATION

In the half-lit dawn, tense with the undone,
I walk my body like the family dog
Three times around the hospital parking lot
Chanting beneath my breath in the early sun.
Roosters compete with the ventilators' hum,
Cool breezes, motorcycles, a new fleet
Of color-coded nurses, while around me
Old women sweep my curling path with brooms.

In the corner, ignoring us, his back turned,
A man in uniform lights joss sticks, feeds
The spirit house with its unlit Christmas lights,   *saan phraphuum*
Uneaten fruit. As he walks back to the ER
A bulbul sings. Just then, for a moment
I am filled with the lostness of being anywhere.

10/10/03; 7/26/04

FOR JINTAPAK

I ask you, "Why do you want to come to America?"
"To work ten years, enough to make some money
Then I come back, build a home for old
People who have no families, nowhere to live.
My husband thinks I will never pass the exam.
'You should live well in your life, not in your dream.'"
And when your brother was killed, and your father died,
You adopted a son, so your mother would not be lonely.

All this I learned as your English teacher, slowly.
Right off, a brand-new pen-pal in Manitoba
Has learnt you are a fan of Britney Spears,
That you were when young in southern Thailand
Twenty years a beauty queen (you liked it!).
Have I lived too long inside this brain?

10/14/03; 11/11/03

FOR SHARON DAHL

"In the hills of South India, by a waterfall,
I sat for two hours in deep samadhi
Aware of nothing. Then I opened my eyes:
Someone had left money in my lap.
In fact, this happened again. The second time
I looked in my lap and there was a banana."

Riskily mindless, you were frightened twice.
Once in Varanesi, you followed a man to his shop
And when you had finished buying, it was hard to leave,
And dark, and you had trouble getting back.
"Another time, three of us were in a car
It was night, and we were stopped by dacoits."   *highway robbers*
"Dacoits! But they kill people. What happened?"
Again – this is interesting! – you don't remember.

10/26/03

For Hans Peter Roth

It's different, having circled round the world,
The lightning flashes searing storm-black Aceh,
The Andamans, Goa's coastal lights,
Oman, the terminal brilliance of Dubai,
The blackness of Arabia and Iraq,
To my host Hans Peter I've never met
Whose chalet overlooks the Thünersee,
Cowbells, clouds, glaciers, the Jungfraujoch.

When I was last here in 1950, all
These snowy spruces seemed far from Quebec.
Now time and the world both shrink. We talk again
Of Rudolf Steiner and the unborn child,
Empire, 9/11, Skull and Bones,
The quest for justice again mystical.

Hotel Rothorn, Schwanden, Sigriswil, 10/30/03

Note: Of this exceptional storm it was reported a week later that 200 people
had died in flash floods, caused in large part by illegal logging with the
connivance of local troops and police.

RECALLING V-J DAY, 8/15/1945

Into the dawn, the raucous pent-up crowds
Danced and embraced along St. Catherine Street,
Strangers were partners in a different world.
At peace, the future would set us free,
All things be possible. But what we celebrated
Was our omnipotence. No enemy
Was in sight, so some youths instead,
Laughing, burnt a small Chinese laundry.

Torn white shirts of peace – they served to flag
The mindless revelers. I was sixteen.
Did no one see these banners as a sign
Of our karma, what Yeats missed, the proud bomb
By which we were made victors, and betrayed
As soon this tenuous morning star will fade?

10/5/04; 4/21/05

WRITING A FRIEND'S OBITUARY FROM XI'AN

For Czeslaw Milosz, 1911–2004

From Xi'an, Czeslaw, I email back my words,
I was changed by you. You taught me to seek the timeless:
Li Bai's poem in the script of Mao Zedong
On the palace wall beside the steaming pool   *Huaqing Hot Spring*
Outlives Mao's Xi'an pact – or the pact of Yalta,   *1937–45, 1945–89*
That consigned your nation, and thus changed you as well
To be just a poet, and translate from far,
Like Xuan Zang, who went abroad from Xi'an   *602–64 C.E.*

And then returned, sooner than you, with sutras
That survive to this day only through his Chinese,
As you returned with the book of Job in Polish:
One world, one Internet, with words that to survive
The beacons of war on Horse Mountain Li
Must change with us: *thy neighbor as thyself.*

Xi'an, 12/6/04

Some notes for Western and Thai readers: Background can be found in the *Song of Eternal Sorrow* by Bai Juyi (772–846), recording how the infatuation at Huaqing of the Tang Emperor Tang Minghuang (685–762) with the beauty of Lady Yang Guifei (also celebrated by Li Bai on imperial command) led in 755 C.E. to chaos and rebellion. Huaqing Hot Spring, where Tang Minghuang ordered Lady Yang to bathe, is at the base of Lishan or Black Horse Mountain, half way up which Chiang Kai-shek was captured in 1937 and forced to sign a pact of cooperation with the Chinese Communists against the Japanese. Thus Lishan was involved in the downfall of three corrupt rulers: King You of Zhou (fl. 781 B.C.E.), who played fatal games with the Lishan beacon, Tang Minghuang, who abdicated after the An Lushan Rebellion of 755 C.E., and Chiang Kai-shek. (Note that Tang Minghuang is more contemporary with us than with King You – an observation which as a teacher I used to make about Dante and Virgil.)

The Yalta agreement of 1945 (from which Chiang Kai-shek was excluded) ushered in a half century of nervous world peace; but it also ceded Poland to the Soviet Bloc. This led to a Communist government in Poland, and the subsequent lengthy exile of Milosz to Berkeley. I completed and emailed my rushed obituary remembrance of Milosz at Xi'an on December 6, 2004.

BIBLIOGRAPHY

Paul Mariani, *Lost Puritan: A Life of Robert Lowell* (New York: W.W. Norton, 1994).
Carol Shields, *The Stone Diaries* (New York: Penguin, 1995).
Dirk Van der Cruysse, tr. Michael Smithies, *Siam and the West, 1500–1700* (Chiang Mai: Silkworm Books, 2002).

IV

For Maylie Scott

FOR MAYLIE SCOTT (KUSHIN SEISHO DAIOSHO)

(March 29, 1935 – May 10, 2001)

i

At my seventieth birthday party
you came with Howard, whom I, not sure
of the right word, introduced as your friend.
It was easier to have you there with him
easiest of all to have you there in a crowd
so we could be friendly and not dwelling on
our intimacy gone.

How different, on your death bed,
when I felt, if anything, closer than before
when we were still difficultly married.
And I knew, even though earlier I had never
believed in an afterlife, that I would soon
be following you into that other zone, on which
your strange eyes were already focused, where
the past will be, is,
more present than the present:

apricot-picking in the Okanogan
all week long walks to the store and back
to the low bunkhouse where we cooked our suppers
(young hitch-hikers – who could have guessed
you a Radcliffe girl would become an abbess?)
or how I used to sweep you up and over
barbed wire fences, until in time you told me
not to do it, you'd rather fend for yourself –

this flashed on me, as we carried you,
sheet-bound, downstairs to your coffin.

ii

Parking the car in the snow
I struggled down through dense thickets
till I came out at a broad farm.
No news of you! I traveled back by subway
and not knowing which stop to get off at
if I was ever to find my car

I woke up. What is most surprising
is to be haunted by dreams again.
All of us sharing more and more vivid dreams
while you yourself went deeper and deeper
into that other world where eyes
in the ceiling beckoned and black shapes called

as decades ago, flattened as never before
by hepatitis, in the London hospital
I saw in the ceiling of the darkened room
the face of my grandmother in black
who herself before she died had told me
of the spidery fingers beckoning to her, "Come!"

and before that in Paris, before I met you,
those days devastated by too much freedom
I could not cope with, so that nothing happened,
those nights still vivid, as when in a lane
I discovered, wrapped in glossy butcher paper
what I knew to be my grandfather's bones

and again last night, back in the run-down
summer boarding-house, I ventured into
the ladderless root-cellar, where they handed down
unwanted discards, parts of a broken cello,
and I saw the effigies of two ancestors
their heads shaped from tear-encrusted sand

and saw when waking how this waking world
will begin, like ice floes in an impatient ocean
as now for you, to crack apart, drift elsewhere,
and then vanish, yes, like a dream.

iii. Trust

We first learned to trust each other skating
when we laughed at the deep rumble of the ice
as it adjusted to our bodies' weight.
We forgave each other that expensive dinner date.
and went on to hikes high into glaciers,
the waterfall we climbed in your eighth month.

Near the end I brought you to the Lost Coast
where we swam among the sea lions,
even after one of them, too friendly,
sent you scattering out of the water.
It seemed best when we lived like that, simply,
left the skillet out on the beach for the fox to clean.

Afterwards you settled here, far from the haunts
of your father's six-course dinners in Manhattan
for the intellectuals and doctors
of the Rockefeller Foundation, one of whom
dabbled in mind control for the CIA,
a brilliant culture you so came to question

you'd block the tracks of a munitions train
or camp in the desert to obstruct a test.
Preferring the simple practices of Zen,
you ignored the colonoscopy,
the science which promised your mother at 55
a chance to live five more years, and gave her forty:

not wishing to be too concerned with life,
you prepared for death, and were ready for it,
leaving me, less trustful now, still clinging
to the peaceability of that moonlit night
in the Marble Mountains, when we both woke up
to the bobcat, inches from your moonlit face.

iv

Your white naked back was turned towards me
While with your over-the-shoulder glance you beckoned,
Now no longer a partner, an oneiric guide
To places beyond you, where my eyes
Saw only darkness.

In that darkness your short-bobbed hair
Was still secular, not yet shaven;
Your eyes, enticing me by dark arts
You always, we always, had a bit of,
Put me in mind of the panic

Of that first frightened dinner together,
Fears that diminished, as you came into the house
Where my father, with his hands outstretched
Discoursed, after his crisis, upon that world
He had hoped to change.

And now, of two minds, while I do not budge
From my father's familiar tracks and habits,
You still visit from that other world, your eyes
Darknesses, riven at their center
With uncertain light.

v

You turned the veggie "meat loaf" out of its pan.
Parts remained stuck inside. You were embarrassed.
I said, No problem. No one at the table
Neither our children nor our separate partners
Knew what happened next, as secretly,
Eyes meeting over the plate, we covered it
With conspiratorial gravy;

Encouraging you, weeks later, to come back,
And say to me, this showed how we could still
Share things, make things happen. You wanted me
Merely to speak out at your nuclear protest
(You knew it was not my wont to get arrested);
But as it turned out

You had planned it for Shabbat, it was no problem
(*Lo kasheh*, a term in Aramaic
I learned with Ronna from our Torah Study)
For me to decline, as in any case I would have,
But still I was aroused by the seduction,
The secret, I now see, of your beguiling
Backwards glance towards me in the dream:

The mischievousness we heard Baker Roshi
Talk about at Green Gulch, on that Sunday
(*The Zen tennis player still wanting to win*)
When our marriage was already breaking up
Like Zen Center itself, although we did not know it
(*By not knowing we enter the way*),   *Ryokan*

Or the rush, years earlier, from hillside sex
Outside Quaker City (with its awkward climax
Of footsteps, questions, a ride in a patrol car)
To the gray-frock-coated wedding in New York,
Children, my increasing lecture trips,
Your hair shorn, separation
We could not keep up with,

So now in your face, over the "meat loaf," close,
Too close, illicit, inscrutable,
I saw for a moment what will always
Intrigue, elude my western mind, a glimpse
Of what we chanted in Old Japanese:
The Sutra's puzzle: *form is emptiness*   *Heart Sutra*

The glint to which each failed moment beckons.

vi

Six red-faced newborn cootlings skim the lake
like windblown cottonwood. Their mother surfaces,
drops scattering off her back, to feed them
beak to tiny beak.

In a week, both they and Elizabeth Maylie
also red-faced at her birth, have grown
larger, calmer, though she still turns her mouth
to suck at my sleeve.

Alan last summer at the memorial,
Imploring Maylie, "Where are you?
Among the buddhas of the western paradise?
Or here waiting to be reborn?"
My son, having just shared with me his news,
Gave me a nudge.

The drops scatter off the mother's back
Just as the cootlings, three now,
each large as my fist, scatter.
And then return.

MARIANNA

(Poem to my first grandchild)

Buddha face you will quickly lose
for a face like the rest of us
a mask of self

what is it you remember
that composes you
to look so serenely inward?

With my own children I thought
weighed down by self-importance
of what I could give them

now as my mind empties
I see it is you
who give to us

We stare in amazement
as your newborn breaths displace us
nudging us towards that silence

where the long line of children
who in their turn became parents
prepare a space for us

All we ever spoke for
has come back to infancy
the predestined past

Commuting to the Land of Medicine Buddha

COMMUTING TO THE LAND OF MEDICINE BUDDHA

For Denise Levertov, d. December 20, 1997

i

It did not bode well
we arrived late and
even before sitting for the first time

knew from the path through the meadow
now widened to ruts and roadway
that those redwoods with fatal
blue crosses on their trunks
had been carried off

East of the creek
old logging trails once
closed with brambles
now brightly ticketed
with red nylon ribbons
brow log   skid trail

Trying to be here
but already plotting
my early escape
to Denise's private memorial
while listening half-attentive
to my teacher's instructions
on what to notice

I returned to the dark wood
in my threatened mind
and recognized trails
opened for a different
catastrophic purpose
were nonetheless serviceable

even if alien

ii

A commute retreat!
driving back each night
to a hot shower
and warm glass of illicit sherry
at the Blue Spruce B & B

silently we would wind up
the music-box flannel Santa
on our double bed
in the Two Hearts room

iii

This sequence of events
while sitting eyes closed
against the dawn light
in the tall armchair

the sound of brushing
pop of plastic bottle
seltzer poured in a glass

and then the commotion
shifting over
from my right to my left

the soothing of linen
a zipper zipping
something placed gently on the carpet

is my wife

a series of pulses
scientists tell us
even an electron is like that

iv

By the third day
a twinge of rebelliousness
at having to let go
of daydreams more enticing
than the blankness in front of me

Gary Snyder arriving
to give tonight's lecture
relaxes for a few minutes
by lighting up a
Groucho Marx cigar
with a Groucho leer
until the thought police
rush out of the *gompa*   *temple hall*
to tell him *this*
is a non-smoking area

I complain
If I bring my attention
to this I will never find out

what happens next

v

Our teacher gives us
A Buddhism of faith
without belief-systems
the Pali for *faith*
being the same as the word
for *hospitality*

but outside   in this valley
of doomed redwoods
being cut down by our hosts
to pay for *the Preservation*
of Mahayana Buddhism

the rituals of Tibet
(Thomas Merton says
the Vipassana methods
are simpler than the Tibetan
and go less far)

the great Tibetan prayer wheel
of 64 billion miniaturized
*Om mani padme hung*s
with printed instructions

Simply thinking of a prayer wheel
helps a dying person
to shoot the consciousness up
to reincarnate
in the pure land of Amitabha

When frustrated
I give it a sullen turn
the equivalent of years
of meditation

vi

Up ahead in the shadows
of a giant redwood
I thought I was clever to discern
the dark silhouette
of a sharp-shinned hawk

but in a moment
he swooped straight down towards me
larger and larger
then curving off to the left

where I could now see the fine
striations of his soft belly
and then in a few seconds
something unheard of
he dove at me again

he could have knocked off my cap
had I not been clutching it
to protect my clenched averted eyes
remembering pictures of new-born
lambs blinded by vultures

a clear hawk-will
against that of an ironic human
uncertain what he is doing in this wood

one part of me burning *to not*
deny experience
a curiosity stoked
not just from love of science
but even more from romance

Dante Inf. 26.116

(this was like a test
as of that knight in *Yvain*
who from good sense turned back
and missed the great adventure)

wishing to wait for the fairy-tale
third attack of the hawk
when I would hardly be surprised
to hear it talk with instructions

But the other part concerned
if I were not an invader
just like those other men
he must have already seen
condemning the trees with blue paint

(or as when a child at Lachute
I walked in and then ran out of
the windy pine wood
having seen there my mother
and her bohemian friend pegi
both half naked)

made the decision I instantly
had to regret
that this place is his not mine
not to be violated

I left and the next day
I could not return
because of the violent rain

vii

This indecision
the flight of a bird
just as my thought changed course
recalls my dilemma
about Denise

I had promised David
to come out in mid-retreat
for the private memorial service
then for the first three days fretted
perhaps only from fear
of the drivers and highway patrolmen
on New Year's Eve

I phoned to break my promise
and for the next three days
was again obsessed
I will not be there to commemorate

the one day she and I
walked down in the forest
over huge fallen logs
to the heron beside the lake

the invisible mountain

her faith like mine
shrouded in doubt

viii

The theme of this retreat
after all by now
my general out-of-placeness
unable to follow
the teacher's instructions
I had to let go
to focus by default.

on my thin breath
writhing in front of me
against a dark veil
now inward now outward
as sinuously as smoke
from an extinguished candle

ix

The early series
of *Ox-Herding Pictures*

Losing the Ox
Finding the Tracks of the Ox
Riding the Ox Home
concluding with
Forgetting Oneself and the Ox

and the two later additions
Returning to the Source
Returning to the Marketplace
with Gift-Laden Hands

x

thoughts without end
a series of pulses
on New Year's Eve
here in the Land of Medicine Buddha

and also in Berkeley
where I failed to join them
reading you Denise
wholly present to the beneficent
swansdown grace of a single night

your breath
now in so many places

xi

Sunlight after rain
the wet hazel branch
studded with rhinestones
changing colors
on which a winter wren
appeared to sing to me
a hint of Nibbana   *Nirvana*
that was aesthetic
but when I went down to
the darkness of the creek
(not necessarily in this order)
the still thisness of the straw
on the logging road
under the redwood droppings

was what you
in your doubting religion
might have called holy

xii

We left early
not very much resolved

but a week later
in New York for the memorial
to James Laughlin
along with you Denise
the last two survivors
of the world I used to write for
older than myself
now no longer here

I found myself
at the Met exhibit
of Degas' family pictures
auctioned after his death

in the midst of my breathing
unable to distinguish
between the thisness
of the faces in the portraits

and in the crowd

VI

THE WINGS OF TIME PASSING

For Yang Xiao and Anna Xiaodong Sun

As we sipped our port
while looking at Rilke and Zhuangzi
with our Chinese and German dictionaries
my mind associated
perversely back to the Oporto
Symposium on East Timor

so I mentioned Byron
how Ronna and I stayed at Sintra
in the Byron Room
with ancient hand-painted wallpaper
the hotel once a palace
where (I found out later)
Byron wrote *Childe Harold*
in the front courtyard

and you, Yang, who did not know Europe
said something like, *Things like that
never happen to us.*

But then you were lost in thought
and after a few moments' silence
recalled how in your distress
after Tienanmen
you withdrew by joining
an archaeological expedition
to the Buddhist Temple
where the Tang poet Bo Zhuyi
took refuge after the eighth-century
time of troubles.

and we all were quiet
as I felt envious
imagining that cliff I shall never see
in the gorge of the Yangtze Kiang.

But now that you are at Middlebury
I look back to the excitement
of our tentative exploration
the heady perspective
where we might have been the first
after reading Zhuangzi Rilke
as they were always destined to be read

that is together

THE TREE

He had driven her
to the famous writer's funeral

where she stricken with grief
at the dull sound of the earth

hitting the hollow wood
clung to his side like a vine

closer to him than ever before
in twenty-four years

The notables looking at them
From across the open grave

may have thought they were lovers
as indeed half of him was

one side chilled, dragged down
with the gravity of death

one side lightly, deliciously aflame

He had seen a tree like this once
on the university campus

the north side dulled with a few brown leaves
the south side dappled green

in blossom

Thailand, 1/6/05

THE RIDDLE

What is it that made my building
in the far north of Thailand

sway backwards and forwards
sent a ten-inch wave to San Diego

drowned three hundred fishermen in Somalia
countless thousands in Aceh

sent my wife to Krabi
to help calm the shrieking

where a mother recognized
(among the five hundred corpses

stacked in the makeshift morgue
of a Buddhist monastery)

the bride's body black bloated
bursting its bikini

identified by the inscription
inside its diamond ring?

and inspired Thai TV
to show an excruciatingly beautiful

video of tourist Thailand
peasants flailing rice

chao na

fishermen casting their nets
in steep-cliffed rivers

chao le

as done for thousands of years
followed by the urgent wave

up a village street
pushing cars refrigerators people

and then the body-bags
slung from carrying poles

coffins lifted over the debris?

To those of you farther off
and tempted to explain this

as *earthquake* or *karma*
can you recognize the riddle

that awakened us with a scream
words won't answer?

Thailand, 1/4/05

DIFFICULTY

pour J.L. Erick Pessiot

One night when he admitted
how he was difficult

he told me his story
living alone with his father

till men who called themselves *maquis*
came at night and took his father away.

At the funeral someone nudged him
and said *That woman over there in black*

is your mother

Then he lived in an orphanage
on wartime rations

of which an older boy always took half
until one morning

in the vegetable garden
he felled the bully with a spade

The boy was never seen again
not a word was said about it

forget the stars and planets
forget punishment and justice

forget death which should instruct us
but makes life difficult

can we dream of a republic
in which people will be able

freely to tell their stories
and the dark silent secrets of novels

will dissolve into candor?

It was a story (in his words)
  de gamins jusqu'à quinze ans
  qui ne savaient ni lire ni écrire

the maturing of language
    beyond Virgilian fate
  Dantean aspirations

the discovery of ourselves

Thailand, 1/6/05

PLEASURE

When I was a very young man
    I liked falling in love:
  no two loves were alike.

Later, in the mountains
    I loved building fires for my children:
  no two fires were alike.

And at last, a meditator
    I glimpse the delight of breathing:
  no two breaths are alike.

EARTHLIGHT

There are moments
when disasters of hurricanes and floods

connivings of small men with great power
the unspeakable sufferings of the powerless

even our climate once natural
now more and more intemperate

are seen as they have been seen in our lifetime
from the near side of the lunar landscape

and sometimes perhaps by all of us
with some imagination

as earthlight

CAPE FLATTERY, WASHINGTON

Purple aster, goldenrod
Push through the buried sands of my northern childhood
The sands of this glacial parking lot.

Across the strait, the fog is banked like snow
Against the blue sides of Vancouver Island
Not foreign to these Indians; they, unbothered
By foreigners' arrangements, still intermarry
Trade across the water, hold potlatches.

Beyond this cape, the last island
With its uninhabited lighthouse.
The viewpoint guide lends me her binocs
To see where a single puffin dives below us
And when the gulls scatter off the tidal rocks
Points to the cedars, from behind which, in a moment,
An eagle will emerge.

Rain-heavy cobwebs hang in the Sitka spruce.
"This is the end of America," I say,
And she, a full-blooded Makah, smiles,
"Or the beginning."

The fragment of Schumann from the next room
almost as faint as the memory
of Frank at our old upright piano
back in the thirties. My heart
is moved, gently. I turn to you
napping beside me, in preparation
for the century's end tonight, and say
"I used to hear my father play this
fifteen years before you were born.
It's been a long road."
And you say, "To the right place."
Yes. We hold each other, in silence.

Tonight, at Mike and Charlene's
on Grizzly Peak, we hug again on the deck
as we watch the tiny fireworks bursting
in the blurred fog over San Francisco
ten miles off. Muffled booms
as after a thunderstorm
which has stopped being scary
and arcs like the white smoky trails
of the forgotten tear gas
we once saw all around us
right here in Berkeley.

The others come outside with their elegant
half glasses of champagne. Below us somewhere
young people cheering.

12/31/00

NON E COSA IN TERRA

the piano music
louder and louder
so completely beautiful
that even when I woke up
and could no longer hear it
I went on feeling the pleasure
that could only have come
from something inside

and when I went back
to seek out the piano player
on the floor above my office
the guard at the back door
had a smaller than human head
disguised by an animal mask
with short purple fur

She said *If you come in*
to your office by this entrance
of course you will have to pay
(because of the piano festival)

and then after the two
simultaneous weddings
held at different football camps
under the auspices of friends
(Alan Williamson smiling)
I found the small room
in which the bride was waiting
with her circle of Tarot-reading
much older bridesmaids

and I said to her before catching
the minute irritations
where she had shaved her legs
You are the only beautiful person here
Don't embarrass me she said
in front of him

and I said (not fully
believing it at first)
He is just a figment of a dream

you are all just figments of a dream

PELICAN

The beak is skewed
    belly bloated like an old man's
  feet buried in the wet sand

but our slow approach is stayed
    by the small eye   open
  blinking slowly once or twice

not from terror
    but in some bardo where   *interim death-realm*
  there is much to contemplate

a distance making it
    closer to us near death
  than was possible in life

After the tide goes out
    we walk back along
  this fall shore that smells of dying

we know what it means
    when we see the priestlike crows
  the raven strutting as we walk up

the devout vultures
    that will not stir
  even when we stare down at them

round their raw bloody dish

I have to remember
        over this glass of chardonnay
    as I suck and squeeze the elegant

claws of this fresh cracked crab

WHAT IS BEAUTY?

"For real men and women also fear beauty, and fear to be beautiful."
– Duval

We are subjects, not objects ...

yet how can we escape
the trace of beauty
in the deepest darkness of who we are

as in the silence
and depth of your *Samadhi*

wrapped from head to toe in your sari
even your face covered

to keep out the predawn cold
as you sat on an abandoned temple ledge

above the Ganga at Varanesi
in such complete concentration

you ignored the faint *tssst sssts*
gathering around you
over every inch of your silk

till you opened up your face
to the warmth of the lifting sun
and first felt on your skin

– yes! this moment of fear,
not yours in your stillness,
but mine on hearing this –

the cockroaches

rich, wild, beautiful
in the dawn light

as your own dark hair
before it is brushed

WORDS TO DU FU FROM THE OAKLAND AIRPORT PARKING LOT

At the airport to pick up the guest speaker
words fail me. High overhead
what you heard as your gut froze
the creak of geese flying north   again

奧克蘭機場停車場與杜甫言

機場迎遠客
無語聞雁至
聲聲寒入骨
又是北歸時

Translation by Anna Xiaodong Sun
Transcription by Yang Xiao

KINGFISHER

ahead of our canoe
the blue flash
of the kingfisher

diving under a wave

MENDOCINO

For Angela and William Young

In a world where, even on calm days,
Surf breaking makes sea-cliffs shudder,
Tide-tunnels deepen in search of new stacks,
Where a mere shift in temperature
Will with the aid of water
Exfoliate even granite,

After life's labors, you deserve this calm
Above the ocean, on this lookout point,
Ferns, asters underfoot, and the osprey's shadow,
A place to gaze from, and to be at home

Above where crows feast on a pelican,
Cormorants scurry across the spindrift
To their perilous perches,
In any weather.

VII

A SIMPLE, DIFFICULT, LESSON IN THAI

Extracted from Se-ed's Modern English-Thai Thai-English Dictionary

Phra in Thai means *monk*. It also means *God*. Or *Buddha*.
so when you *wai* a monk, it's like *wai*-ing God   *bow in respect to*

Usually God is *phrajao*, and Buddha, *phraphuttajao*
(Buddhists don't believe in God? Tell that to a *chaophut*!   *believer*
                                                in the Buddha

         i.e. to myself   to disturb
         the lightness of my own meditation)

One same word for monk and god
is a big leap for an American. Not in Thai.

Phra also means hero, as in Phra Ram
the *Ramakian* hero, and Phra Lak his brother   *Thai Ramayana*

And *phrajao* can mean *lord*, or *king*
or even (this may surprise you) a *king's head or hair*

And *phraphuttajao* is a title for a king   *Phraphuttajao Luang*
who is always called Rama.   *(Rama V)*

         candles, incense, families praying
         at the statue in the park
         of Phayao's first king

the enchantment of the male nurse
with a college degree:
The most exciting moment of my life?
I was seven in Chiangkhaem
and the king went by in a motor car

In the *Phrabarommaharajawang*

(Or Grand Palace) is the Wat Phra Khiaw,
the Emerald Buddha Wat, with 178 murals

showing Mount Krailart, Phra Siva and Lanka   *Shiva, Sri Lanka*
from the *Ramakian*, as written by Phra Rama I.

I have gone there twice. I live in Phayao (far north
from the capital city, or *phranakhon*)
in the *Lanna* country, not really part of Siam   *Million Rice-fields*
till they built the railway in 1921.

The *phra*s that I see every day
are the *saan phraphuum*, our hospital's spirit shrine   *earth-spirit*
                                                                      shrine

the monks with their alms-bowls
outside the 7-11

and in the sky above us
phraaathit, the sun, *phrajan*, the moon

daophrasuk the morning star

the eye of the cobra

BREATHING EXERCISE: A HOW-TO POEM

For Gil Fronsdal
and in memory of Mark O'Brien (1949–1999)

The distance between the brightness
at the top of the spine
and the darkness below it

is not far
but when you shrink your mind
it is enormous

the whole length
of human history
can be fit inside it

One way to reduce it a little
is with practice and preparation

(the latter takes minutes each morning
the former has taken me years)

to gather the sensations in our belly
into our in-breath

(do this slowly and with enjoyment
the darkness deep inside us
should be like the jungle in Thailand

where we may acknowledge the presence
of unseen pythons and kraits

but our actual sensations
as we search the deep canopy
for crimson sunbirds

are of lazy butterflies
and flowering lianas)

and then by a skilled relaxing
of both muscle and nerve
guide our breathing

slowly up the back of our spine
so that it breaks over the top
like a wave breaking over a quiet beach

to drench the scattered thoughts
spread out to no purpose
and then draw them slowly back down

in the descent of the out-breath
to the dark easy rhythm

of the untiring diaphragm
where the in-breath began

Relax the spaces in between
each vertebra
let each space slightly expand

until in each out-breath
you can exhale *metta*   *compassion*

commingling the cool light
and warm darkness

to those whom you usually consider
enemies and friends

NO THIRD WORLD

America, you need to hear it
There is no *third world*

which is barely disguised code for
what in the fifties we confidently

named *the underdeveloped countries*
meaning *not like us*

But there are many *developments*
I more developed

at solving cryptograms
and my wife, at deciphering people

America more developed
at exploring outer space –

where we see our own orb
as did St. Benedict   *Greg. Dial. 2.35, 4.7*

a bright milky pearl

and Thailand at giving –
both rich and poor at dawn

lined up to place food
in the begging bowls of the monks

at the edge of the highway
There are many *developments*

America certainly more advanced
at developing email

Burmese at the mental development   *bhavana*
which enables monks to read minds

Tibetans at curing cancer
with Precious Pills at the new moon

and Haitian dancers at walking
across hot coals without being burned

many yangs many yins
but if I had to choose

I would go with the *Tao Te Ching*
and aspire

to the condition of water   *Tao Te Ching, 8.20*

GOOD-BYE TO THAILAND

i

SAWNG THAEW

In the back of the *sawng thaew*   *two-bench pick-up taxi*
(with Ronna gone to Bangkok)
I am just four feet away

from the young Thai woman
on her motorcycle
hair bravely flying

eyes fixed firmly on the road
I think *you are Thailand*
not knowing whether you are like

the rice-growing villagers
who yesterday filled
the backs of their pick-ups

with blankets mats power saws
huge tureens of coconut curry
for the monastery *katina*   *gift-giving ceremony*

or more like Ronna's students
who gape up
at the cafeteria TV monitors

with their ads for laundry soap
or skin whitener
and in the intimacy

of my foreign language
reinforced by the taxi's noise
I call out *I love you*

as you continue down the road
and I turn off to the left

waving good-bye

ii

LEAVING PHAYAO

I walk past the large classroom
of students in clean white shirts
furiously writing exams

I was once one of those students
once the invigilator so worried
someone in the room might cheat

I was once the professor
sitting bored at the desk
reading a newspaper

more years than I can remember
and now I am an emeritus
like the old men I once thought irrelevant

not yet having known this freedom
to be the only one
watching the purple heron

drift slowly north across the sky

SECULAR PRAYER

Our will be done!
Not your will and mine
but *our* will be done

moving out beyond
our selfish combative elements
like St. Augustine in the garden

his bones clamoring   *ossa clamabant St. Aug. 8.8*
for *nothing more than*
the will to go there   *nihil aliud quam velle ire*

but a will that is resolute and settled   *fortiter et integre*
made easier as St. Thomas said
by our common *appetite for the good*   *Aquinas Ia2ae 94.2*

until *to commit injustice*
rather than suffer it
is the greater misfortune   *Plato Gorgias 509C*

our will not Christendom's
as in Jerusalem long ago
when *the Muslim and Jewish population*

men women and children
were massacred
by the victorious crusaders)   *1099 C.E. Cambridge History I, 196*

not America's will
(Fallujah's *thermobaric*
fireball consuming oxygen

for *enormous overpressure*
people *literally crushed to death*)   *Guardian, 11/22/05*
not the mindless will of civilization

converting Akha mountaineers
after the forests have been clear-cut
into *plantation labor*   *www.akha.org*

not the will to power
of our leaders corrupted
by gold and *ostrich eggs*   *Brown 16–17*

not of the naysayers
uprooting language
from the dark sky of *mythos*

to the mere daylight of *logos*
(like Freud's cocksure
We leave Heaven

to the angels and the sparrows   *Freud 50*
assigned for freshmen to read)
nor their opponents dissolving

satya or truth (from Old English
trēowe　　firm true
Guide us in the straight path)　　*Ih'dinas Sirataal mustaqiim Qu'ran 1.5,*

Cf. Psalm 5:8, 27:11, 86:11, 143:8

into mere fables
and the irrelevant dumbed-down poetry
supported by affluent empire　　　　　　*Saunders*

If the leaf venations
of trees now threatened
show reticular development

since the Cretaceous　　　　　　*Boyce and Knoll 72*
will we not also
be capable of refinement?

What matters most is unrecorded
as political structures crumble
into complex unity　　　　　　*Whitehead 31*

the great entropic river
whose course we pray is certain
beneath the surface setbacks

from contrary winds and tides
and the mere self *a shadow
cast by grammar*　　　　　　*Wittgenstein*

176

And thanks to common endeavor
from Nestorians in Baghdad
Byzantines in Renaissance Rome

Danzig refugees in Cromwell's London
or in our lifetime
Tarski Arendt von Neumann

tribes on murderous frontiers
may someday join with us
in googling for pure pleasure

and all will be meaningful
not a phrase of our communication
that is meaningless   *Duncan 218*

I will pour out my spirit on all flesh   *Joel 2:28*
but because impossible received
in some places less   *Paradiso 1.3*

while a few
Milosz Snyder Levertov
may someday be remembered

for their unstylish faith
in old words like *transcendence*   *Levertov 103, Milosz 254, Snyder 39*
and the unununderstood

(*to tell of* ▉▉▉▉ *is not possible*   *Greg.Naz. 27, 40*
thereof one must be silent)   *Wittgenstein 7*

Whether just lost in a forest
or at the end of another empire

(both have happened before
on the long homeward path)

the river is one
and the crowds in the airport

for the delayed plane
are one fleeting moment

no longer misshapen
each person radiating

a rich particular story

NOTE

gold and ostrich eggs: St. Cyril of Alexandria bribed the emperor's court with
gold and ostrich eggs (and much more) to confirm the banishment from
the church of the Nestorians, many of whom sought refuge in Persia and
China. By analogous maneuvers the African Donatists were also excluded,
explaining their later swift conversion to Islam.

See Charles Freeman, *The Closing of the Western Mind: The Rise of Faith and
the Fall of Reason* (New York: Knopf, 2003), 215–16, etc.

BIBLIOGRAPHY

St. Thomas Aquinas, *Summa Theologica*.

St. Augustine, *Confessions*.

C. Kevin Boyce and Andrew H. Knoll, "Evolution of developmental potential and the multiple independent origins of leaves in Paleozoic vascular plants," *Paleobiology*, 28. 1 (March 2002), 70–100.

Peter Brown, *Power and Persuasion in Late Antiquity: Towards a Christian Empire* (Madison, WI: University of Wisconsin Press, 1992).

The Cambridge History of Islam: I. The Central Islamic Lands (Cambridge: Cambridge University Press, 1970).

Robert Duncan, "Towards an Open Universe," in *The Poetics of the New American Poetry*, edited by Don Allen and Warren Tallman (New York: Grove Press, 1973).

Sigmund Freud, *The Future of an Illusion*, in *The Standard Edition of the Complete Psychological Works of Sigmund Freud*. Vol. 21 (London: Hogarth Press, 1968).

St. Gregory of Nazianzus, *Oration 27*, translated by Frederich Willimas (Crestwood: St. Vladimir's Seminary Press, 2002).

Denise Levertov, *New and Selected Essays* (New York : New Directions, 1992).

Czeslaw Milosz, *To Begin Where I Am: Selected Essays* (New York: Farrar Straus and Giroux, 2001).

Frances Stonor Saunders, *The Cultural Cold War: The CIA and the World of Arts and Letters* (New York: The New Press, 1999).

Gary Snyder, *Earth House Hold: Technical Notes & Queries to Fellow Dharma Revolutionaries* (New York, New Directions, 1969).

Alfred North Whitehead, *Process and Reality: An Essay in Cosmology* (Cambridge: Cambridge University Press, 1929).

Ludwig Wittgenstein, *Tractatus Logico-Philosophicus* (London, Routledge & Kegan Paul, 1974).

ACKNOWLEDGMENTS

I wish to thank the publications in which versions of the following poems first appeared: "The Power of Prayer," "Wittenham Clumps," in *Brick*; "Occitanian Spring," "Something Precious," "Holy Land I: Truth," "Holy Land II: Force," "Confession," "Making History, Unfolding World," "The Size of Earth," in *FlashPoint*; "Mae Salong," "Wat Pa Nanachat," in *Conjunctions*; "The Tao of 9/11," "Cape Flattery, Washington," "Turn of a Century," "Mendocino," "Words to Du Fu," in *Jacket*; "Above Siberia," "Bangkok Reunion," in *Epoch*; "View from Phayao Ram," "For Carol Shields," "For Raquel Scherr," "Jacques de Coutre (1595)," "For Sharon Dahl," "The Tao That Can Be Expressed," in *Chain* 12; "Luzern Symposium: Der inszenierte Terrorismus" and "Recalling VJ Day, 8/15/1945," in *nthposition*; "Marianna," in *Alaska Quarterly Review*; "Christmas Retreat: Commuting to Medicine Buddha," "Difficulty," "Non E Cosa in Terra," "Pelican," "Kingfisher," in *Heyoka Magazine*; "The Wings of Time Passing," in *New England Review*; "The Riddle," in *Only the Sea Keeps: Poetry of the Tsunami*, ed. Judith Robinson, Joan E. Bauer and Sankar Roy (New Delhi: Rupa & Co., 2005); "A Simple, Difficult, Lesson in Thai," in *The Literary Review of Canada*; "Breathing Exercise," in *Queen's Quarterly*; "Good-Bye to Thailand" (i. "Sawng Thaew," ii. "Leaving Phayao"), in *Yale Review*; "A Ballad of Drugs and 9/11" (earlier versions of "The Tao of 9/11"), in *Lobster* and *FlashPoint*.

I owe a great debt to the Lannan Foundation and its helpful staff for the chance to write for two months in West Texas, and to make new friends in Marfa and Fort Davis, as well as Santa Fe. I owe a great debt also to our circle of friends in Phayao, Thailand, particularly our generous hosts Terry Kong and Thanis Kanjanaratakorn, MD. I wish to thank my friends Yang Xiao and Anna Xiaodong Sun

for their help, including Anna's translation of one poem into
Chinese, and Yang's transcription of it. I also wish to thank Susan
Burgess Shenstone for her help, and in particular for contributing
the "Renvoi" to my poem "Occitanian Spring" (about our shared
experience of over a half-century earlier). My thanks to Paul Almond,
Bryan Sentes, Jasper Bernes, and Florence Elon, for their assistance
in final preparation of this book. And I cannot say enough about my
debt to my circle of poets in Berkeley, two of whom in particular,
Chana Bloch and Alan Williamson, have been most helpful. In both
my life and my writing, my debt to my wife Ronna remains, as always,
immeasurable.

TO RONNA

The trees here in Claremont Court are red.
The lake at Naresuan was blue.
I have been so very happy traveling these past years.
But only, my love, because of you.

February 14, 2008